# THE PROCESS OF POETRY
## EDITED BY ROSANNA MCGLONE

First published December 2023 by Fly on the Wall Press
Published in the UK by
Fly on the Wall Press
56 High Lea Rd
New Mills
Derbyshire
SK22 3DP

www.flyonthewallpress.co.uk
ISBN: 9781915789143
Copyright Rosanna McGlone © 2023

The right of Rosanna McGlone to be identified as the author of this work has been asserted in accordance with the Copyright, Designs and Patents Act 1988.
Typesetting and cover design by Isabelle Kenyon, imagery Shutterstock.

All rights reserved. No part of this publication may be reproduced, stored in or introduced into a retrieval system, or transmitted in any form, or by any means (electronic, mechanical, photocopying, recording or otherwise) without prior written permissions of the publisher. Any person who does any unauthorised act in relation to this publication may be liable for criminal prosecution and civil claims for damages.

A CIP Catalogue record for this book is available from the British Library.

This project has been supported using public funding by the National Lottery through Arts Council England.

*To my mother*

# CONTENTS

| | |
|---|---|
| Preface | 7 |
| Don Paterson *The Sicilian Advantage* | 10 |
| John McCullough | |
| *I've Carried a Door On My Back for Ten Years* | 20 |
| Victoria Kennefick *Choke* | 30 |
| Pascale Petit *Ortolan* | 40 |
| Sean O'Brien *The Reader, After Daumier* | 50 |
| Hannah Lowe *The Register* | 60 |
| Regi Claire *Extract from (Un)certainties* | 68 |
| Gillian Clarke *The Piano* | 80 |
| Kim Moore *All the Men I Never Married No. 42* | 88 |
| Caroline Bird *The Final Episode* | 98 |
| George Szirtes *How to play Your Internal Organs Overnight* | 108 |
| Liz Lochhead *Chimneysweepers* | 118 |
| Mona Arshi *The Lion* | 130 |
| Jacob Sam-La Rose *Credit Due* | 138 |
| Joelle Taylor *Extract from C+nto* | 146 |
| *ROUND SIX the body as haunted house* | |
| Biographies | 154 |

# Preface

No poet publishes a first draft, at least, not until now. Invariably, what you see are carefully honed words, nurtured into being, but what goes on before those words reach the printed page? From my own experience as a poetry tutor for many years, it is clear that most writers have little awareness of the skill and stamina involved in crafting a poem.

This was the motivation behind what you are about to read. '*The Process of Poetry*' offers an opportunity to explore early drafts by fifteen of the nation's leading poets and to hear the reasoning behind their development.

These poets have been the recipients of numerous awards including the TS Eliot Prize, The Forward Prize for Poetry, The Costa Book of The Year, The Eric Gregory Award, The Creative Scotland Award, The Queen's Gold Medal for Poetry, Foyle Young Poet of the Year and The Wilfred Owen Award. One has been the Scottish Makar and one has been The National Poet for Wales. Several poets have work on school syllabi. Moreover, their expertise extends beyond poetry and includes editing, publishing, judging, translating, lecturing, and overseeing spoken word events.

How was the project undertaken? I approached a number of poets whose work I admired, poets who come from highly diverse backgrounds and represent us all. I was aware from the start that they would need a willingness to make themselves vulnerable in order to share their expertise.

Initially, each contributor sent several poems, from which one was selected which best exemplified their craft. Some poets offered very early drafts, or even journal notes, whilst others provided later versions still in need of improvement. The aim was to showcase a wide range of writing styles and redrafting techniques.

A series of interviews was conducted, enabling each poet to discuss the development of their work, some of which is based on traumatic events. Whilst a few writers have given a broad overview of their working methods, others have chosen to focus on the minutiae. Some have analysed single words, others a change to title, subject or form. It is these interviews which form the basis of this book.

The aim of this project is not to identify and scrutinise every single alteration in each poem.

The book raises a number of questions. Where does a poem originate? How do you decide on a title? When do you choose the form for your poem? What are the best approaches to editing your work? When would additional input help? How do you know when a poem is finally finished? What should you consider when assembling a collection? What is a publisher seeking?

Contributors have offered their guidance on the skills that a working poet requires, entering competitions, translating and writing for performance. Whilst often their advice concurs, I love that it is, occasionally, contradictory. I trust that, as a reader, you will respond to the variation that is presented and take away with you what is most helpful.

My hope is that this book will preserve the unique insights and materials of living poets for the next generation. Better still, that the value of this undertaking will be recognised and that there will be an opportunity to expand it more widely in the future.

Thanks to Arts Council England for their support with this project and to the Hosking Houses Trust for providing a residency in Stratford-Upon-Avon, during which some of the initial work was undertaken.

**Rosanna McGlone**

# DON PATERSON
# THE SICILIAN ADVANTAGE

## *The Sicilian Advantage (Early Draft)*

For me? You shouldn't have. No, I mean it.
I hate surprises. But this is nice, thanks.
Not sure how you found out but anyway.
I'm no a self-celebrant   . don't celebrate myself.
back against two walls, eyes on the door and the fire exit.
here at Clio's - 90 degrees. Corner table.
Yes, my usual table. My only table.
in the corner see them coming  Yes I'm here most every night these days,
with the vitello Milanese and the house chianti.
Please don't say *creature of habit*. Saves cooking, thinking.
that's not what this is about. It's control. not because I'm cheap creature
of habit / safety / saves thinking. four doors down at 35 / I almost shot
him dead Ah you found me. Can you move one inch to your right?
Thanks.
They show me to my table now, always the same.
Corner table, set for one, back to two walls,
eyes on the doors and the fire exit,
and never more than 90° to worry about.
I mean you saw my bed that one time.
In the corner, with the pillows in the corner.
But I'm monologuing. (hogging it / blethering) . but Please, finish your

## THE PROCESS OF POETRY

boring story

Just keep your fucking hands where I can see them.


You know what they say — those that we admire —
the rich; the smart; the sophisticated —
you imitate them, if you want to be them.
If you don't  ,            you'll be them.
Please keep your hands where I can see them.


and move a little as you're blocking the door
I have my own back, thanks.  back to two walls, I have everything covered
and am unlikely to be surprised, honey.
Hello generally this is how I position myself
The wall has my back /I have my own back
but different / not that anyone is looking for me
But to face only one quarter of the world
As an expert simplification / To face only 90° of the world
I hate surprises /And the last time my stepkids try to: one
Tried to pull that I think it was my birthday

## *The Sicilian Advantage (Final Version)*

For me? You shouldn't have. No, I mean it.
I hate surprises. But this is. Apropos.
Not sure how you knew but anyways,
thank you. Yes I'm here most nights these days
with the house red and the vitello Milanese.
Don't say *creature of habit*. Makes it sound lazy,
it's an economy. No more for me no –
it's okay, don't fuss. I'll have Ugo clean it.
Yeah, same table, parked here like a rook.
Au cont, it's more like my idea of freedom –
you remember my bed that one time, in the nook,
the pillows in the corner. *God* no. Never.
But tell me about your weekend or whatever.
Just keep your hands up here where I can see them.

## Can you tell me how the idea for the poem arose?

I never really know where a poem comes from, other than a vague, chaotic instinct that there's something there to write about. For me, writing the poem isn't quite the aim in itself. It's a bit more weirdly circular. I use poetry as a means of finding out what it is I think and what I want to say in a poem. I'm trying to find out a truth, that's all there is. It's quite close in sensation to remembering something important that you've long forgotten. And then you dig it up and try to write it down in memorable language, so you don't forget it again.

Sometimes there might be a couple of words you start by obsessing over, or two things that you feel go together somehow, but don't yet know how. In this case, I was fascinated by the phrase '*the Sicilian advantage*', and its mafia connotations. My wife always looks for the place for me to sit in a restaurant in a corner, where my back is against the wall, so I can see all the doors. I'm paranoid in repose.

## How many drafts did the poem undergo and which is this?

You want to *look* as if it didn't require any effort, but that wouldn't be very truthful. I write loads of drafts, though way less than I used to. Perhaps thirty for this particular poem. The version you see here was a very early one.

## Let's explore the way in which the poem has developed.

I think of writing poetry very much as a process, and I wait to see what emerges from writing the same material over and over again. I used to like to begin with too much material, but I found I could easily over-compress things, so now I try to keep each draft to the length the poem feels it'll be. That way it works as an editorial constraint. I'm constantly asking myself what really deserves to stay in, and what isn't earning its keep.

When I read the early drafts, I'm trying to be led by instinct to tell me what the poem's crucial elements are – the things with energy, the things I should get obsessed with. I make a distinction between an 'element' in a poem and a 'detail'; the sophistication of the poem is in how the elements interrelate, whereas the details most often work as metonymy, as evidence in support of the poem's argument. I'm also trying to minimise the number of elements or themes, in an Occam's razor way.

I'm just trying to say as much as possible in as few words as possible. If you look at that first draft, you'll see lots of repetition and a lot of detail which really isn't there for more than colour. It's far better to find a single 'telling detail' than clutter the poem with description.

## Although many lines were cut from the early draft, conversely certain words and phrases were added to the later versions.

Once I had the measure of the speaker, I had more of a sense of the things that he would say, the kind of language and shorthand that he would use. He's the sort of dude that says '*au cont*', apparently. Also, by that point, the form was determining most of those decisions. If I'm looking for a rhyme and I know for a fact that he's not only the kind of man who would order the Milanese but pronounce it with a fussy accent on the final '*e*' – this guides or instructs the later rhyme. So I can see I wouldn't have got to '*lazy*' without '*Milanese*'. Yeats used to say that if it wasn't for rhyme, he wouldn't have known what the next line was going to be. There's truth in that.

I can see that at one point in the early draft, I omitted a word altogether. I knew *something* would go there, but at that stage I didn't know what. I do that a lot. I suspect most poets do.

## When did it settle into a sonnet?

The sonnet form is partly a default setting, as I know it from the inside, and it helps me to shape my thoughts more clearly. It's a bit like a twelve-bar blues; you can fill it with a million different things, but it both holds its shape and gives shape to your own thought. It's just a little square box, which asks you to put things of the same kind inside. The symmetry also has a built-in fracture, what we call the 'turn' at around the eighth line. Indeed, it's often the turn which helps me to decide whether it's going to be a sonnet. However, in this case there's only a gentle turn, which is one of the reasons why I wrote it as a single stanza.

This poem is unusual in that it's really a dramatic monologue wrapped up in a sonnet. Through his words and actions, the reader's given some insight into the rather unpleasant personality of this chap. Who I assume is some shadow of me. I guess I felt this might also subvert the reader's expectations. The form tends to be more romantically or metaphysically inclined.

## What are the benefits of the sonnet form?

I use it as an engine to generate language, not just as a way of shaping it later in the process. You want form and content to slowly become the same thing, as they are in music. I want everything in the poem to be magnetised towards its theme – to find the details that evoke the entire scene, the guy's character, the whole relationship with the person to whom he's speaking. So whatever he says or eats or does or remembers should all point to it.

It was important to me to get the other person into the poem. But they could only be present in his replies, his gaps and admonitions and omissions and memories. The more I wrote, the more I realised that I really didn't like the guy, and I suppose I started playing up the darker elements.

The whole sonnet form also acts as a great editorial tool, though. There is an agitation between the language that you *want* to use and the constraints of the form, in terms of line, rhyme, rhythm and length. You don't have enough room to put in everything you might be inclined to.

I also hold this belief that if I can make the music cohere, the sense will too. It's almost as though – if you can just get all the consonants talking to each other, you can make a single word out of each line. This needn't be obvious to the reader's mind, just their ear. But every draft is also trying to work towards that ideal of musical integrity, for all the poem may never get close.

## How did your previous occupations as a professor and editor inform your writing and has retirement affected your writing routine?

Editing and teaching means you have to clearly articulate a lot of things that poets like to leave to intuition. You have to, though, as your job is to say what's gone wrong. Although you learn a lot, making poems can become a much less innocent and more self-conscious act, if you're not careful.

Over the last year, I've retired from St Andrew's and Picador, so my routine has changed — and I'm not sure what it is now. As for poetry, I'm either in a shed in my back garden writing it, or I'm not thinking about it at all. I certainly don't think about poems much when I'm not writing them. I did when I was young, because I had to. Constantly. Now, I might write six poems in a year, or none, but there'll also be periods of concentrated activity where I write a lot. It's a weird cycle. I'll write a book and then the urge will disappear, and then three years later, I'll spot something in the sky like a returning comet, and I'll think — here we go again.

## Is there anything you need to consider before you submit a poem?

When you've finished a poem, stand back and say — if I wasn't me, could I derive everything, every nuance, everything I intended, from just the words on the page? And sometimes the answer is... no. Through sheer overfamiliarity, you end up leaving out details which seem too obvious, ugly and expository, thinking they're still somehow implied. But now it's not in the poem at all. This happens a lot. Ironically, it's the sort of thing that you teach your students and then promptly forget yourself.

## What are the main skills that a poet requires and are they teachable?

The larger skills are to do with their relationship to poetry, and how they configure it within their lives. The smaller ones are mostly technical and quite specific. Whether either set of skills is teachable will depend on what a young poet is reading, and their reasons for wanting to write poems in the first place.

But you can teach anyone intelligent with a facility for language how to write a publishable poem. The basic level of poetic competence has risen a lot, because of the opportunities to learn. Alas, this has a tendency to mask the fact that you still can't teach talent, which is currently drowned out by competence. Talent might still be easy to verify, but it's getting impossible to spot.

But you can teach patience. Cultivate patience, fuel it by
obsession, let yourself become totally immersed in poetry. All
decent poets have been obsessed with poetry to the exclusion
of everything else, at some point in their lives. If you get
obsessed by things, you get better at them through repetitive
practice. And even if you've a smaller talent than someone else,
but you can sit there for three hours longer – you'll end up
writing the better poetry.

## What advice would you offer to emerging poets?

Do it, absolutely do it – but check that you're doing it for
the right reasons. In the first instance, check you're more
ambitious for the poem than you are for yourself as a poet.

If you're not reading poetry, you're not a poet. Identify half
a dozen poets whose work you love, then memorise their
poems. These poets will form your voice as much your own
experiences will. Also – stop trying to find your voice. Any
voice you find probably isn't yours. Voices emerge from our
writing, slowly.

Also try to get your problems down to two: syntax and deixis.
Everything else should be taking care of itself, eventually.

Honest criticism is really important, but it's hard to come by.
Get in with a supportive group of people who know more than
you do and will pay you the compliment of taking your work
seriously enough to comment critically on it.

Anyone who is serious about poetry will seek out a mentor.
Hunt them down and write directly to your heroes. No one
is immune to flattery. The worst they can do is ignore you or
politely decline.

## As an editor for Picador for twenty-five years, what were you seeking?

Well, I couldn't be guided by just my own taste. My job
was to keep the list viable from one year to the next, over
a long period of time. I had no Arts Council funding, only
accountants. But for every book that sold well, I could take a

risk with another that might not. But all I ever looked for was singular talent. Unfortunately, we couldn't afford the staff to maintain a slush pile, so I had to rely on my instinct and the enthusiasm of people I trusted. There's a thriving poetry network out there, and real talent is very rare – so if someone was suddenly writing great poems, it was often brought quickly to your attention, often by several different people at once.

## Who was your favourite poet as a child?

I came to poetry quite late and didn't read any poetry until I was in my twenties and had moved to London to play jazz. That's when I heard Tony Harrison on the telly. And that was that, and the rest is some kind of history. It's Tony's fault. He gave me the only career that pays worse than jazz.

# JOHN MCCULLOUGH
# I'VE CARRIED A DOOR ON MY BACK FOR TEN YEARS

*Door (Early Draft)*


For ten years now, I have been carrying a door on my back.
I watched you lug it once from the builder's yard - solid pine,
rails, panels - and now it's my turn to know its weight,
that press against vertebrae. A decade-long kiss. A door I shut
when I left, when I turned the steel handle and heard the click
of the lock. Goodbye, goodbye, goodbye.

                                                                 Hello.

It is quite rude to take the door with you when you leave
but here I am. I get occasional splinters. It is hard to sit down.
I am always worried about knocking people over, smacking into things.
There is nowhere to put it, no wall to prop it against. It is part of me,
as though I were a hermit crab. There are, however, benefits: I am never
lonely. Doors are never and always in fashion. And people ask if they
can help. I tell them no, walk on, swing suddenly open.

## THE PROCESS OF POETRY

*I've Carried a Door On My Back for Ten Years*
*(Final Version)*


You lugged it from the builder's yard.
Now it's my turn to know its stiff weight,
the slow chafe of pine against vertebrae:
a decade-long kiss, flush with splinters.

I closed it when I left. The lock snicked.
Then I noticed it hitching a ride. It never
gives up—patchy blue, invisible straps;
a faint knocking though nobody's there.

So many slab hazards: repeated thumps
to my skull, brass hinges clouting strangers
as we creep into lifts, beds. I lie awake
on its panels, framing rectangular thoughts,

obsessed by the side I can't see; what grows
there. The problem is you died so there's no way
to set the thing down, no wall to prop it against
with its stuck handle and fracturing paint.

All day we continue our back to front tango,
this dance where I almost but never arrive,
where I'm shut off to visitors for hours
then, with one touch, swing wildly open.

## How does a new poem come into being?

For me, a poem starts from many different routes and it's a long process. There's no programmatic way or everyone would use it. In order to begin a poem, I need to be excited about a subject and keen to unlock something in the reader. I start with an image or a phrase which I want to extend further, in order to unpack its significance. I rely very much on my notebooks, which I comb through to see if I can find a few phrases and look for a thread to connect them.

I'm less successful with idea-based poems. I need a motivating passion or I won't be able to channel the feeling to the reader, which is a key aim for me.

I like electricity in my work, so I'm most inclined to create in the morning after a cup of coffee, when I have high energy levels and am feeling particularly alert. I begin by freewriting at speed, simply to get things out of my head. I like to use sculptured phrases, images, observations from people or specific details from one of the many books of facts that I have.

I also have a passion for investigating language, and words that have become obsolescent, and use a copy of Samuel Johnson's Dictionary, which was first published in 1755, so is perfect for the job.

## How did this poem originate?

I'd written lots of poems on my first partner and his death, when I came across a book about a man who'd carried a door on his back from Land's End to John o'Groats and this striking image resonated with me. Grief is a force which causes people to act in unpredictable ways and the door is an extended metaphor to convey that sense of carrying around unresolved feelings.

## Can you tell us which draft you're sharing with us and how long you worked on it?

I don't really number them but this was a very early draft, indeed probably the first full draft. There's a wholeness and

an overall structure which made it good enough to share with
other people and I remember taking it to a writing group and
receiving feedback from friends. As it was the last poem that I
wrote for my collection, '*Spacecraft*', I didn't have the luxury of
tinkering with it over a larger period of time, as I often do, as I
usually have a three-to-five-year gap between books.

## Let's explore the change in form.

During the editing process, I often try putting my poems into
different forms and structures to see what effects it creates,
and whether there might be stronger alternatives to the shape
in which they were originally conceived.

Here, the final version imposes a stricter form on the subject.
The rectangular stanzas mimic the subject matter of the
'*rectangular thoughts*' but, more importantly, the stanza breaks
amplify a sense of detachment and isolation.

The other key change is that the shorter lines slow the poem
down, so that the reader can linger on the imagery and feel the
sadness within it resonate.

## How important is the title and how do you go about choosing this?

One of the first things you'll notice here is that in the final
version, the rather plain and uninspiring original title, 'Door',
has been replaced by what used to be the opening line. It's very
important to arrest a reader, to make them want to read the
poem, so it's good to think of the title as a vehicle for doing
that, rather than as a purely functional thing. An original,
striking title can really excite someone and put them into a
receptive mood straight away.

## There are a number of word changes in the final draft. How do you choose the right word?

Poetry is about trying to stir emotion in someone who doesn't
know me/you. When I'm thinking about verbs and adverbs,
I ask myself if it's the best candidate for the position. I like
specificity, precision and sensory images, so often replace

something broad with something very precise in a later draft. For example, *'press'* becomes *'slow chafe'*, which is a more sensory image and *'suddenly'* becomes *'wildly'*, which creates an emotional punch because of its contrast with the earlier, flatter tone. I replaced *'click'* with *'snicked'*, as it works much better sonically.

## You change, *'I watch you'* to a direct, second person address, *'You lugged it'*.

Yes, I often strip language away from the beginning of the poem. I want to ground the reader and arouse their curiosity as well as create a sense of impetus and momentum, and I think that the direct address is more immediate. I have used more conversational language as a means of developing intimacy with the reader, rather than employing a more self-consciously literary approach.

## I notice that whilst the metaphor of the door develops to become almost a character in its own right, you lose the image of the hermit crab.

It's important to watch out for competing images which work in opposition and undermine each other, rather than strengthening the poem. Some images may be great as isolated lines, but during my editing process, I ask myself whether the images are working together as a team so that they gain a cumulative power as the poem proceeds. I'm seeking focus and intensity.

Here, although I liked the image of the hermit crab, and was sorry to lose it, it's a tangential image and didn't quite fit with the central image running through the poem and the overall theme.

Stripping the crab away has tightened the focus on the surrounding units and the physicality of the door. This is emphasised further in the final version, with the addition of more concrete details like, *'flush with splinters'*, *'stuck handle and fracturing paint'* and *'blue'*, all of which create a more precise and intricate picture.

**A striking addition in the published version is the line, '*The problem is you died*'.**

Yes, because it was a strong piece, I wanted this poem to work on its own as well as being part of a book. Without this line, there was a lack of knowledge about the reason for the heartbreak. However, this makes it clear that it wasn't simply that we had separated, but that my partner had died which, I felt, was necessary for the reader to know.

**Can poems inspired by personal experience be written for reasons other than publication, and how does this impact on the revision process?**

Absolutely, they are. There's a difference between writing therapeutically with a cathartic aim, where you just write whatever is most helpful for you as the writer, and writing to engage a stranger emotionally, which means making them active. For instance, a writer often doesn't think about making changes afterwards with a therapeutic poem, whereas a poem frequently has to transform the writer's experience fundamentally, if written for an outside reader.

I'd certainly be prepared for a poem to say something that isn't how I see the world. With my kind of writing, there's always a slight difference between the speaker of the poem and the poet himself, even when the poem tries to persuade the reader otherwise. I wouldn't hesitate to change the details of most poems unless I thought it might in some way deeply hurt someone I care about.

For me, there's always the need to have some degree of intensity and passion, but the older you get, the more you run out of key moments to write about, so it becomes more challenging.

**The poem uses a wide-ranging selection of punctuation. Can we explore its importance?**

I love punctuation. You can create a much wider range of emotional effects by using it with precision. I've always been drawn to the individual effects of punctuation marks and their difference from one another. We're encouraged to stick to commas and full stops, but to me the semi colon has a liminal identity between those two and I find them delightful, connecting two sentences which are close in meaning, whilst celebrating the intricacies and variations.

Furthermore, the exclamation mark offers a sense of being outrageous which really appeals to me!

A poem is a structure of silence as much as sound and it is important to spend as much time tinkering with the silences as the sounds. This includes stanza breaks and white silences on the page. I'm keen to have the option to focus on precise pauses, and to determine the length of the pause, and the use of punctuation enables me to do this.

## How do you know when a poem is finished?

I wish I did. To quote Paul Valéry, 'A poem is never finished, only abandoned.' For me, publishing is an arbitrary moment where it's out there and I do think of tweaking my poems further, even years after they've been published. I'm only stopped by the cost of the reprint.

## How important is resilience in the world of poetry?

I like experimenting, even though I'll often produce a failed poem when I try to take a risk. All of my failures and mistakes are necessary. A failed poem, for example, often just requires a different approach/way in. The images and phrases are never wasted and will go back into my notebook for another time.

The majority of my poems don't achieve the necessary structural cohesion, but it's often only through sharing them with others, or submitting them to magazines, that I realise that they're not working. This is an important part of the poetic process.

## In your experience as a lecturer, what are the main obstacles that students encounter?

Whereas I find that an unfamiliar poet can open me up in a different way, energising me and getting me excited about the possibility of language, some students have a barrier to reading what others have written and this is a big problem. Read as widely as you can. Don't circle the same two or three poets, otherwise you will struggle not to sound like those writers.

What's more, sticking with the familiar inhibits a willingness to experiment. We all develop mannerisms over time, but these can calcify around you, and you need to break free of whatever patterns are constraining you. Students become comfortable with particular structures, for example the sonnet, as they know how it operates. Once they've learnt how to write a sonnet, they're reluctant to explore other forms through a fear of failure. People are afraid of making mistakes, but there's no growth in the familiar.

Another common problem is that students can become attached to the first phrases that come into their minds, which are often received language phrases which lack the originality, energy and intensity required to bring the poem to life.

Furthermore, I encourage my students, wherever possible, to go to the place about which they're writing, so that it becomes more experiential.

Finally, in order for your poems to reach a public standard, you need a dogged commitment to going back and forth again and again, working on your approach to technique and structure.

## What are the challenges of putting together a collection?

Nowadays, I work with a collection in mind, focusing on a dominant theme. However, the identity of a collection may change over time. This may require poems to be extracted if they don't fit in with the new overarching identity and the accumulative effect of the central, underlying emotion.

However, that doesn't mean that they might not fit well in another collection, just that poems have to wait their turn for the right book to come along where they'll be at home.

I find it exceedingly difficult to choose the order of poems within a collection. For example, with *'Reckless Paper Birds'*, you wouldn't believe the number of different orders it went through. When I first started, I was trying to hide similarities by keeping them far apart. I kept on and on, as I felt I hadn't got it right. Yet when Tom Chivers, my editor, worked with me on the order, he brought a fresh perspective. Rather than focusing on keeping poems apart, he found pairs that worked together.

## What drew you to poetry?

As a teenager I was very isolated, partly because I grew up in a working-class area of Watford. I was bookish and I didn't have any friends. I was gay, but I couldn't tell anyone, so when I began writing poetry, it was probably more for cathartic reasons and a desire for emotional connection. I wanted to create with other humans and loved the thought of having that effect through my words.

## Did you have a favourite poet as a child?

As a teenager my biggest influences were Sylvia Plath and Ted Hughes. I was fascinated by their very passionate extremes, violent imagery and oceans of blood. Their work switched me on and acted as a sort of gateway drug to poetry, as I wanted to capture those passions myself.

# VICTORIA KENNEFICK
# CHOKE

## *Choke (Early Draft)*


By now, it's clear I have an oral fixation. I want to hold things in my mouth – a key, buttons, a fingernail (click of a boiled sweet against enamel), clog of peanut butter so thick I can hardly breathe. It almost choked me once, the tablespoon I shovelled from the jar. I hacked, gulped firmly, eyes streaming. My face pink. As a toddler I stole my mother's pills, pried the lid off the bottle with my tiny teeth – how did I do that? – ordered the tablets by colour and size. My mother panicked when she found me, drugs skittled on the bedspread. At the hospital the cup of charcoal, its burnt taste, black coming out my mouth into a white bowl the nun held. I thought I must be bad. Full of temper. Maybe this desire to smother, coat my tongue, plaster my teeth is to keep the blackness down. That, or I am hungry. Boiled sweets, being given one as a child by an older cousin, a good girl I offered it to my little sister just as my mother turned to say *no*, she popped it into her mouth, turned a dainty shade of blue. I was banished to wait in the grass with my cousins like the snake I was, convinced I'd killed her. My father turned her upside-down, the sweet shaken loose. In another version, my mother pushes the sweet down her throat with a finger, or maybe that was me when I was three and nearly choked in a (different) cousins' house on (another) boiled sweet. Maybe that's what I'm looking for, my mother's finger down my throat, pushing sugar deep into me. Sometimes (not often) I do that to myself. More often (always) I have my fingers in my mouth.

## *Choke (Final Version)*

    I want to hold things in my mouth –
    a key,

                  buttons,

a fingernail,

                the click of a boiled sweet
against enamel.

        A toddler I stole my mother's pills,
        prised the lid off the bottle with tiny teeth,
        arranged the tablets by colour and size.
        My mother panicked when she found me,
        tablets skittled on the bedspread.

            At the hospital the nun
            held the cup of charcoal to my mouth,
            I spat black into a white bowl.
            Its burnt taste,
            I thought I must be bad.


A child, given a boiled sweet by a cousin,
I popped it in

        my mouth,

turned

        a dainty shade

of blue.

        My father spun me upside-down,
        the sweet shaken loose.
        In another version, my mother
        pushes the sweet down

> my throat with a finger, or maybe
> that was when I was three
> and nearly choked
> in a different cousins' house
> gagging on another boiled sweet.
> Maybe

that's what I'm looking for —
my mother's finger
                    down my throat,
pushing
              sugar
deep into me.

## When did you start writing poetry and what got you interested in the medium?

I've always done it. My family were very encouraging and I was given lots of anthologies to read from early childhood. I've been obsessed with rhymes from an early age and have never forgotten the relief of that shared experience when I've read them, the sense that yes, someone else thinks, and feels, like me.

So much of my impulse to create poems is to communicate. I just love words! They're a great blessing.

## How many drafts did 'Choke' go through and over what period of time?

I began it in 2016 and wrote it over a couple of years, and perhaps twenty drafts. This is roughly the tenth draft. The earlier versions were much longer and more tangential.

## It feels like a very personal poem. How did the poem originate?

I think what I'm really interested in is the idea of a personal poem. As a child I was defiant and intrigued by things I wasn't allowed to touch. A lot of poems in the collection have their origins in memories, photographs and in stories I've been told as a young person. My mother's baby brother died of choking and it's every parent's primal fear.

However, the poem goes beyond this. I was interested in trying to figure out how choking went through my childhood, but also what it meant in a poetic and metaphorical sense. Memory isn't always reliable, particularly when it comes to remembering things as a young child, but the kernel of the story is true in as much as I remember it, the curiosity and the wanting to explore elements which, as a child, were forbidden. The first thing that came into my head when I remember taking my mum's tablets was the nun holding up the porcelain bowl and the charcoal. This was a very visceral memory and the poem developed around that.

## What is truth in poetry?

I suppose there's real truth on a personal level, what actually happened, but then there's poetic truth and I'm really interested in the space between those two realities. There's a point where you, as an individual, have to let go of the truth of the event, to allow the truth of the poem to take over. A lot of the poems in this collection have their origin in personal experience, but are transformed into something completely different where the truth of the experience, I hope, is still there, but is articulated in ways that are more artistically authentic. It's not a confession or an exposure, it's a very crafted, instinctual, but also intellectual situation.

**The earlier draft seems almost like a stream of consciousness. How did it evolve? I am interested too in the shift in focus, so that you become the recipient rather than the giver of the sweet.**

There are a number of things at play in excavating a poem from beneath, or behind, words that shouldn't be there. As a poet growing up, I grappled with the notion of how much you leave in and take out. I used to write very long poems and edit them so much I'd take out the whole poem! This was one of my greatest challenges as a poet. It comes down to trusting yourself, but also trusting the poem.

As I wrote the poem, it bloomed into something very different. Initially, it focused on my guilt at giving my sister the sweet upon which she choked. I was attached to my little sister, as a placeholder, to facilitate me delving deeper into an emotion. It's almost as if I had to write through this, to explore the confusion in a safe place and then distill it. When I shared it with my readers, they asked me if my sister's experience was the poem, so I began to reevaluate and refocused completely on the speaker, removing the conversation around texture and colour which distracted from the process. By keeping the incident, but transferring the choking to myself, it became more disciplined and minimalistic.

**The change in layout is clearly significant.**

The first thing you notice when you see a poem is the shape. The way in which the structure serves the poem is such an integral part of the poem and transforms how it reads. Initially, I was envisaging the choking as a tight knot.

However, I realized that presenting it in this form - choked full of words- was suffocating other elements in the poem which needed to breathe.

It was too dense and the thick text was stifling the message. I wanted to create the sensation of process and food journeying through the throat, but also the sense of the words being almost like steps towards the next generation of being fed.

## A number of the words alter as the poem develops.

Regarding the word choices, I changed *'ordered'* to *'arranged'*, as I wanted to express as precisely as possible what a child does and I feel they have a sense of arranging items, whether this be cars, buttons or sweets, rather than ordering them, which is a more adult concept.

*'Drugs'* became *'tablets',* as the latter has the most appropriate register and reflects the language I would have used. Even pills would have been more appropriate than drugs. I read a lot of American poetry and I think there was a little leakage, as *'drugs'* is more an Americanism than *'tablets',* which is a word that you would find in everyday conversation.

I think it's important to consider including the vernacular in your poems, rather than finding a weighty, more formal word if this works better with the voice of your poem.

## I am interested that, in the later version, the focus changes and the nun becomes the subject of the sentence.

This arose for two reasons. I wanted to get the power dynamic across and was therefore interested in the nun assuming a more active role. She was a figure of authority who was going to persuade me, a three-year-old, to eat charcoal. I wanted to explore how much you impose your authority and will on a child, although, obviously in this case, it may be necessary for their wellbeing.

I used the definite article *'the'* because she represents all nuns, rather like Yeats' swans, they clearly couldn't be the same, but they all merged into one. It was she who, through feeding me the charcoal, could see what a bad girl I was as the blackness came out of me.

Secondly, I felt that some of the initial description of the charcoal was self-evident and therefore redundant. Basically, less is more. The key image for me was the stark contrast between the black (of the charcoal) and the white (of the bowl).

**There are several sets of parentheses in the earlier draft. How do these link with uncertainty?**

As I was writing, I felt that I was second-guessing versions of events that had happened long ago, seeing things from the perspective of others. There was no definitive version. Oftentimes, I'm undermining what I'm saying in a very conditioned way. I find decision-making a challenge. You have a page, and you have words and you have decisions. The stakes, when it all remains in your study, are not high.

Removing the parentheses equates with removing those uncertainties. I was trying to create something cleaner by omitting things I saw as weaknesses. Ironically, in my current work, I'm realizing that those self-same uncertainties could be strengths.

**You stop earlier in the final version. Can we talk a little about that and where it leaves the focus?**

One of the most exciting things for me is finding the final line. When I reach it, there's a sense of relief at tying things up.

However, whilst I love a dramatic crescendo, in many respects 'Choke' ends with an unresolved scenario, as I wanted to leave that *'pushed sugar into me'* hanging. The sense of it being a continuous process of me being fed and being a recipient is implied through the repetition and the hallucinatory quality of the choking. Yet, it's important that there's space for the reader to find their own version of the poem.

**What are your own working methods? Do you have a routine or notebook by your bed or in your handbag?**

No, I wish I did. I have no consistent way of doing things. I've tried, but it caused suffering. I have an instinctual process. One of the things that helps me most, and I very much enjoy, is writing a stream of consciousness, leaving it and moving away from it for a time. So much of writing poetry is learning your process, letting yourself get it all down.

Afterwards I always read my poems aloud, and record them, so that I can listen to them and identify what works and what doesn't.

## Earlier you mentioned your readers. How important is feedback to you?

I initially wrote all of these poems in a very private place, as I think we all do, and it was around six months before I could move beyond the preciousness of the poem and on to the craft. Reading it in preparation for someone else reading it, you suddenly see it very differently, because it's no longer yours and that initial creative impulse and protectiveness has transitioned into a more analytical approach. There's a big relief in that and it leads to a greater openness in redrafting.

I wanted support with the process and was incredibly lucky to have feedback from Rebecca Goss, Collette Bryce and my editor, John McAuliffe, who are all working poets and can swivel from creating, to providing an analytical approach to my work. It's very important that you find a group of people whom you trust, but who are also sensitive to *your* poetry and want to help you to find the most crystalline version of the poem.

They helped in subtle ways. They never told me what to write, but rather posed questions which encouraged me to reflect on my work and find the solutions for myself. Rebecca enabled me to see that you don't have to put all of your ideas into the same poem. Instead, you can save words, or fragments, to use elsewhere.

## *'Eat Or We Both Starve'* was your first collection. Can you tell us a little about putting this together?

What I found interesting in writing the poems for the collection was the arrangement, through the chaos, of images, themes and research. It was slow and confusing and like walking through mud. Yet, it was important to me that the end result was clean and crisp and focused. The struggle was working out the impetus. What is inspiring me? What am I interested in?

I wanted the poems to stand alone, but equally I wanted there to be thematic links between them, without compromising individual poems. What happens to individual poems when they become part of a collection? It's important that they stand individually, but also whisper, shout and hold hands with each other across the collection.

## As a creative writing tutor what advice would you give your students?

Be open and receptive to what is being presented. It's very useful to have a notebook or a notetaking app on your phone to jot down stimuli. These could lead to nothing, or alternatively they could become a line or a whole book.

Everyone has their own little habit that they struggle with. Write your way out – or in – to it, but whatever you do the most important thing is to have fun! Ultimately, it's the process, not the end product.

If you want to publish a pamphlet or chapbook, give yourself the time to step back. For your own well-being, have a safe distance between the act of creation and the end product. This time away will afford you fresh eyes and a new perspective and, by sharing your work with a trusted reader, you will definitely benefit.

Finally, I would say that it's important to develop a thick skin.

## PASCALE PETIT

## ORTOLAN

*Ortolan (Early Draft)*

```
1st draft    Ortolan                    30/12/13.
When the doctor says it's only a matter of weeks
                      an
my father orders makes the arrangements. A chef
is brought in, the bunting still spring in its cage
singing, the cage covered. It has been in the dark
                         sigs and
for a month, fattened on maize. My father
listens, while the the Armagnac is poured into a bowl
and the bird is drowned alive. He thinks the silence
                                            its death
will be like this: a sudden silence
                    a singing in the dark
then a sudden silence, while the tiny (gold and green)
                     flesh
feathers of his body are plucked, his feet
                                          snapped off.
Eight minutes he waits while the Ortolan roasts
feet in a ramekin, then it's brought to his mouth,
almost burning his lips. The chef
                He's paid for
                A white napkin is draped
over his head for the brandy vapours to envelop him,
and to hide his shame greed from God, who he does not
                                            a         believe in.
but who knows Bird in the mouth
          places the whole
He eats the head first, crunchy the crispy skull red
the flavour is like divine.
                                       hazelnuts
the yellow fat melts, the bones are like almonds.
Five years he has sung been in his dark cage home
```

# THE PROCESS OF POETRY

*~~it singing~~, growing thinner, despite the oxygen*
*rich ~~tubes~~ feed. In his chest his lungs ~~are bloated~~ have ~~strained~~,*
*and his heart flutters, ~~like a luminous songbird~~.*
                                    *mute*
*around the ~~fluttering~~ mute songbird of his heart.*

## THE PROCESS OF POETRY

### *Ortolan (Final Version)*

When the doctor says it's just a matter of weeks,
my father arranges to have a chef brought in
with an ortolan still singing in its cage.
It's been blinded for a month, fattened on maize.
Father watches while Armagnac is poured in a bowl
and the bird plunged in and drowned. He thinks
that death will be like this: a singing in the dark
then the pop of a few last bubbles, while the
olive-gold feathers of his body are plucked,
his feet snapped off. Eight minutes he waits
while the bunting roasts, then it's rushed sizzling
to his lips, a white napkin draped over his head
to envelop him in vapours – the whole singer
in his mouth, every hot note. The crispy fat melts,
the bones are crunchy as hazelnuts. When
the bitter organs burst on his tongue in a bouquet
of ambrosia he can taste his entire life – heather
from the Kabylie mountains, Marseille's salt air,
lavender from Provence – he's flying through
high clouds to his nesting ground. Five years
he's been confined to this small room, grown thinner
despite the oxygen-rich tubes, his lungs
burning around the mute songbird of his heart.

## What was the inspiration for the poem?

I clearly remember writing 'Ortolan'. It was one of those poems where I know what led to it and I remember exactly when I wrote it. It was a postcard from the famous Australian poet, Les Murray, while I was in Paris. In it Les said that President Mitterrand lived on the same street where I was living and that his last meal was an ortolan. Coincidentally, on a previous writing retreat, I had lived just round the corner from rue Ortolan and had no idea what it was. In fact, I thought it was someone's name. When I googled it, I discovered that it was a bird and the highly ritualistic way in which it is killed and eaten.

## How long did it take to write the poem?

Unusually for me, this poem almost wrote itself. I vividly recall pulling out the postcard in the early hours of the morning, during a sleepless night on a little mezzanine in Paris. I wrote the poem in bed in the early hours, doing a few drafts in long hand, and finished it at the table later that morning. Then, I did some more research, in order to find out specifically what ortolans taste like, in order to be able to explore where they may have come from which, fortuitously, married in with the places my father had lived. Having not eaten it myself, I had to conduct detailed research as I wanted it to be as real as possible. Once I had the research material and the image in my head, I could immediately transfer it to my father.

## You explained that at an early stage you considered writing it in three stanzas. What led to the change in form?

I wanted to create a tableau, almost a sculpture, where the man has the cloth over his face. If you had it in three stanzas, there would be respite for the reader and the form would be artificially broken up. It wouldn't be a single white napkin anymore, so it's crucial to have it as a solid block of text. I had this image of the single white cloth draping over everything, which lends itself more to a solid block of text.

**I notice that there are a number of omissions in the final draft.**

Many of the omissions were as a result of me trying to take away the extraneous material, paring it back to the absolute bones of what was needed to tell the story without being austere. In my early notes, the napkin was *'embroidered'*, however this was irrelevant. White works better for so many reasons, for example, the sense of purity.

There is conjecture about why they put the white cloth over the head, either to keep the flavour in or to hide the guilt from God, however ultimately, *'Hide his greed from a God he doesn't believe in'* was really moving on to another subject and was a distraction from the installation at the heart of the piece. I wanted to keep the poem in its trance, focused on a very intense last meal. I don't know if my own father actually ever ate an ortolan, but it felt right. *'Flying through high clouds to his nesting ground'* and the bird is a heavenly thing which replaces it.

In the fifth line down, *'My father'* loses the personal pronoun becoming *'Father'* in the final draft. I work very intuitively so I tend not to analyse why I'm doing anything. A lot of it is to do with the tune, the music of it, so it might have been to do with not wanting an extra syllable. I didn't say *'Papa'*, which is even warmer and what I sometimes call him, but didn't do so here, where there's a certain coldness and formality; perhaps I'm distancing myself from his actions.

**You change the focus from your father listening, to watching, and create a visceral picture.**

Yes, while I use *'hear'* and *'watch'* a lot in my poetry, I'm a real watcher. Substituting *'watches'* for *'listens'* gives a more filmic image and heightens the sheer horror of seeing the bird drown in front of you.

Having not eaten an ortolan, I looked it up and had it really vividly described, so those details come from my research as I wanted it to be as real as possible. I think the imagery becomes more sensory and visceral, so *'A sudden silence'* becomes *'the pop of a few last bubbles'*, *'are like'* becomes the visceral, *'crunchy as hazelnuts'* and the ramekin is, *'rushed sizzling to his lips.'* It was important to me that it felt authentic and as real as possible.

## It's interesting to see that the line, *'Eight minutes he waits'* moves from the beginning to the middle of the line putting waits on the end.

The sentence straddles the line break, so the reader's eye rushes ahead to find out what's coming next, but because you have an unnatural line break you have to go over it, there's an unnatural pause there, you can't rush to the bunting. There's definitely an enforced pregnant pause after *'waits'*, to take in the process that the father can't avoid. I don't want it to come to a full stop as the process hasn't ended at that point, so there's no relief for the reader either.

## How do you approach writing about difficult relationships and events?

When my father, whom I hadn't seen since I was eight years old, reappeared when I was forty-two, I knew that I had to write about it, it was a big subject, but for nine months I couldn't. I had a complete block, because I was trying to write it in a realistic way, what his dingy flat was like, and it just didn't work. It was only when, one day, I walked into the Ménagerie in the Jardin des Plantes and pictured us as animals, that I felt I could do it. I'd recently twice been to the Amazon rainforest, so I had that inside me really, waiting, and I just found a way of using those experiences to write about my father.

I had written about my father previously in my second collection *'The Zoo Father'*, but you can't keep writing about the same thing. In between I wrote about my mother, a nature book, the Frida Kahlo book and then I felt I could go back to the subject. *'The Zoo Father'* was an angry book, and I felt I was now in a place to write more compassionately, which I did in *'Fauverie',* in which 'Ortolan' appears.

## What are your strengths and weaknesses as a poet?

I love doing research for poems and feeling that I can make them more real. Quite a lot of my poems come from found images, and many are ekphrastic.

I haven't really tried many set forms as I really love free verse and have a lack of interest in anything that's even remotely mathematical! I attend a lot to the music in my poems, but I do it intuitively. I ask what does this poem want to sing? It's usually other people who go through it and scan it and say that's an anapaest and so on.

I think that my subjects are quite limited. I can't write how I really want to write. I would like to be able to write more about love and joy and to describe the natural world as if it is the first time you have ever seen it, which is a big ask.

Also, I have a tendency to overcomplicate. I'm a maximalist, which can be both a strength and a weakness.

## Do you have a particular writing routine?

Yes, I do. I certainly had quite a specific routine when I was doing a lot of teaching in London which, while a great thing to do, was quite demanding and took up most of my creative energies. I literally did my writing in month-long retreats in Paris, three or four times a year. I would rent a room or a flat in the Latin Quarter. When I wrote 'Ortolan', it was after I had won the Manchester Poetry Prize, so I could afford to stay in that flat in rue de Bièvre, the street where Mitterand had once lived, for two whole months.

I'm very disciplined and focused. I often can't sleep, so I would write through the night in bed with a cup of tea, or at my little desk in the early hours of the morning, before breakfast. The afternoons would be for editing, perhaps after a visit to the zoo or a museum. I really focused and ignored all but essential emails, to which I would respond between 8-9pm. I found that this really worked.

Ordinarily, I would work on two or three poems at the same time. Usually, when I'm writing well, I work in several notebooks at the same time while the energy is there.

I used to share, but now I tend to hang on to a poem and put it away until I feel I can go back to it. Now, I only discuss my work with my husband, who isn't a poet, but who is a real reader, and he tells me if he thinks it's lost its life or what might be unclear.

## What brought you to poetry?

I always wanted to be an artist when I grew up and as a child my natural gift was drawing, but when I went to the Royal College to do a Sculpture MA, my drawing wasn't approved, so I lost confidence in it and became a sculptor.

I was always writing though, and wrote when I was a teenager, especially when I discovered Keats's 'Ode to a Nightingale'. The otherworldliness of the poem, combined with the death and the sickness, drew me in. It's about being human, but it's also a very mystical poem that humans are more than their bodies. It was as if a voice was saying, 'This is the world you belong to.' I would go into my room and do schoolwork or draw or write. In fact, at that stage, I was better at short stories than poetry. I wasn't the best at poetry, I was only the second best, which I didn't like being.

## What have you learned not to do over the years?

One step that was important to me was the discovery that when I'd written my first draft, it was better not to edit it, but rather to rewrite it from scratch, or maybe with a couple of lines from the original which are most alive. I would ask myself, 'Am I really saying what the poem wants to say, or am I making do because it's quite good?' I made a leap in my work when I discovered that you probably have to recast a poem, rather than just edit your initial draft until it becomes okay. Maybe you will find that it's not enough and that you need to begin it again in a different time and mood when you have more energy.

## How do you see the role of research?

Don't be afraid of research, but it should never be dutiful. *'It has been in the dark for a month'* was originally driven by my research, as I had discovered that ortolans were literally kept in the dark prior to being eaten. However, I'm just feeling my way in the first draft, so later this was taken out and replaced by *'it's been blinded'* as it was no longer important that they blackened out the cage, but rather the effect on the bird. Though they may even sometimes blind them too.

You should always be absolutely obsessed and fascinated by the research you do and follow your excitement, because if you're not excited, your reader won't be excited either. With my research for 'Ortolan', although the process is terribly cruel, I found the descriptions very exciting because they're so detailed, and I could clearly see that the bones were *'crunchy as hazelnuts'*, although that wasn't explicit in the research material.

# SEAN O'BRIEN
# THE READER, AFTER DAUMIER

### *The Reader, after Daumier (Early Draft)*

This is the afternoon. It isn't over.
If a train goes by, far off, there will be others.
Light falls through the green, becoming gold
And as it shifts / back once /again from gamboge into olive
[It] makes light of you, and you seem close
To vanishing but never do.
There in the orchard where you sit
There are no plans
 [and in']The orchard where you sit,
And read and wear that wide white umpire's hat,
Although the games's too frantic for your tastes, though to your mind the game's
The fruit unfallen and the page not turned,
Has made /There are / Acknowledges no plans.
*Phaethon* of which a half a dozen lines survive
Completes itself between two sentences.
Your grandchildren will call you soon,
But soon does not arrive. This is
The life, the only life, you wrote.

## THE PROCESS OF POETRY

## *The Reader, after Daumier (Final Version)*

*i.m. Alistair Elliot*


If a train goes by, far off, there will be others.
This is the afternoon. It isn't over.
Light is falling through the green, becoming gold,
and as it alters once again makes light of you,
and you seem close to vanishing but never do.

The orchard where you sit and read
and wear that wide white umpire's hat
has made no plans, while *Phaethon*,
barely half a dozen lines of which survive,
completes itself between two pondered images.

The grandchildren will come and call you soon,
but soon does not arrive. This is, you wrote,
the life, the only life,
here between nowhere and never,
the fruit unfallen and the page uncut.

## Can you tell me about the origins of the poem?

Yes, there were two things which inspired it. One was the death of a dear friend, Alistair Elliot, who was a remarkably well-read man, a leading translator of the classics and a much-admired poet. The other thing was that I was looking at a book of Honoré Daumier's pictures and the one that absorbed me was 'A Man Reading in A Garden'. It depicts a man with a big white hat, sitting in an orchard reading under a tree and the state of active rest was quite suggestive. I was interested in the grey, green, gold coloration and the pale hat.

The poem is ekphrastic in the sense that it refers to things present in the picture. But it isn't a detailed inventory, and is as much about the event as conceived in the imagination of the beholder. However, it's also an elegy celebrating the life of a friend.

## How many drafts did you write and over what period of time?

This poem came relatively easily in four drafts written over a couple of days, but this is by no means always the case. Some poems take a year and numerous drafts. I was lucky in that I'd begun to see the shape of an internal arrangement of the poem that might work. I'd been offered a way in, and the task was to discover the terrain. All kinds of things feed a poem in ways that you're not necessarily deliberately taking note of at the time.

## It would be good to learn about your writing process.

The first draft is just ideas as they occur. It happens that what I write is rhythmic, before any further degree of organisation goes on. The diagonal lines are self-interruptions noting possible alternatives and the square brackets query whether a word or phrase is staying in or going out.

One thing that I find important is trying to establish the climate of the poem, that is, the setting and a suggestion of mood, often in relation to time as well as place. Having the raw material, but in a very unformed way, I then begin to look for shape, and as well as the visible world and its relation to time – which is both in motion and arrested – I begin to look for musicality.

**It's interesting to see that the line order changes on occasions.**

I think what I was doing in transposing the first and second lines of the poem was seeking a way to establish something in the distance that can be apprehended from 'here'. In this case the train came to mind, so there was motion and also the sense of time passing.

The whole poem hinges on the sense of time being both in motion and arrested – because the tribute to the figure in the poem relies on the idea that he is both gone and present. Back in the first stanza, the figure is definitely there, but with a few more tilts the figure in the painting, who represents Alistair, could almost disappear into the background. So, it looks as if light is *'making light of you'*, as *'light is falling through the green'* works in two ways, both making nothing of you, but also illuminating you. In the painting itself, you have the manifestation of light. The poem depends on a series of paradoxes.

The change in the order of the final stanza may have arisen when I got *'uncut'* with a short vowel with a *'t'*, which invokes a kind of faint vowel rhyme with *'wrote'*, a long vowel with a *'t'*. I'm pleased that it's not a perfect rhyme, as it gives the sense of something which is enduring but, in some way, improvised.

*'Uncut'* replaced *'turned'* – which allows lots of overtones – the fruit unfallen, the page uncut, so that the book is not yet finished, if we think of it as an old-fashioned book where the pages need to be cut. This seems to lend the object, the scene and the figure of the reader a sense of permanence, or, as it were, provisional immortality.

## Some of the vocabulary changes and some lines are omitted completely.

It's important that a writer's position isn't fixed. A word choice might work in the first place almost as a sensation and then you realise why it might be apt. Conversely, sometimes you sit there and something suggests itself to you so you try it out and it might work, or it might not. If it doesn't work you always know, even if you're not quite at the stage of admitting that there's something wrong. I really like the word '*gamboge*' and I'm just waiting for an opportunity to keep it in a poem.

'*Falls*' changes tense to '*is falling*' to reflect the continuous process of the event. Even though it's describing a picture which is finished to the imagination, it's something that's still happening.

I changed '*shifts*' to '*alters*', as the latter has a kind of lightness to it that '*shifts*' doesn't. '*Shifts*' is a bit weighty like scene-shifting and I just wanted a lightness of touch, also it's Latinate, unlike '*shifts*'. Furthermore, '*alters...makes light of you*' fits the soundscape better by emphasising the 'l's and 'o's.

'*Sentences*' becomes '*images*' which is obviously much better, partly because it contains 'ages', which is a useful accident.

The personal pronoun '*your*' to describe grandchildren changes to '*the*' because it's a more familiar usage – people with grandchildren say, 'The grandchildren will be coming', not 'our grandchildren'. Also, there are two significant uses of '*you*' just following and if I'd put '*your*' grandchildren, this would have taken the charge out of it.

Some commas are removed from the second stanza, but there is a pause in the middle which strikes a balance between the fact that there's no need for any plans, this is it, here in the orchard, but on the other hand here he is working away on a translation of 'Phaeton'. It's another paradox where something is seemingly concluded and yet he is going on working.

## How do you know when a poem is finished?

There is a sense of something having fallen into place, and simultaneously a fading of the anxiety that the piece isn't finished. There is no longer the same sense of obligation to keep turning it over. Instead – if you're lucky – there's a feeling of resolution.

Yet not all poems are finished. There are certain exclusions where I know that there's something wrong, but I can't identify what it is.

## What does intertextuality add to a poem and does it bring difficulties of its own?

My view would be that the poem has its own life to live and readers are welcome to come and explore it, but you can't expect a poem to explain itself. Its job is to be what it is and do what it does, which means that some poems are necessarily difficult. With experience, we learn to differentiate between a poem with inherently difficult subject matter from one that's just not very well written. Poetry is as real to me as anything else. It has the same authority as a lamp post or a table. It's real and inherent, not merely decorative. You are part of a succession of people who have been pondering the same issues for thousands of years and it's perfectly natural to refer back to something which has shed light on them or been memorable. Much of our literature is allusive to, and dependent on, other works.

## Poetry is clearly a significant part of your life.

I think about poetry pretty much continuously. I'm aware of the fact that it's in my mind very much of the time, so I'm often at my desk working on something and I get very uncomfortable if I'm not able to do that. I still think about poems when I'm on holiday. Why would you go to Japan if you weren't going to write about it? Writing has to satisfy some kind of imaginative necessity. I'm interested in the dramatic life of the poem, the sense of something being offered in three dimensions to the reader's imagination.

Since 2016 I've been working at a greater speed which, I think, has something to do with mortality.

## With whom do you share your work?

For 30 years I've run The Northern Poetry Workshop. We used to meet in person, once a month, but since the pandemic we now meet on Zoom. Everyone sends out a new poem once a month and we have a relatively technical discussion about them. I'm fortunate that, in addition to this, my partner, Gerry Wardle, has read almost all of my work. She has a very good ear.

## Can we explore putting together a collection?

What has tended to happen over the last twenty years is that at some point the work I'm doing has begun to seem substantial enough to think in terms of a book. There are certain recurrent themes in my work: place, history, politics and I am also interested in the workings of the imagination as a subject in itself. I might roughly list poems and consider if each is predominantly about one of those categories. However, the categories aren't fixed. Then I print them all off and consider whether they belong together.

Larkin advised a good strong poem to begin and end and plenty of variety in between. It seems obvious, but the challenge is in choosing. My latest book, *'Embark'*, ends with a diminuendo, but there are lots of ways in which it could have been organised.

At the very start of my career, between 1976 -1981, I wrote a book's worth of poems and it was a case of finding a publisher who was interested in publishing them. Fortunately, Bloodaxe, which was a relatively new imprint at the time, offered them a home, which was very exciting. On that occasion there was a certain amount of chronology to the ordering of the poems, but this hasn't necessarily been the case with other books.

You hear talk about how individual poems should speak to each other and I'm not quite sure what that means, but I feel that they shouldn't get in each other's way and so there needs to be a 'rhythm of design' – which is a bit mysterious, and I don't claim to understand it.

## What advice would you give to emerging poets?

The fact that something is true doesn't make it interesting. Nothing in anybody's background or experience guarantees that a poem will be worth reading. People often refer to their poetry as being personal, as if this somehow makes it an exception to all kinds of judgements that one would ordinarily make, when poetry really has to be the best written thing of all.

You have to know the distinction between writing poems and being a poet. If it's more important to be a poet than to write poems, you may be barking up the wrong tree. Your imagination is the one which is given to you: then you have to discover all sorts of musical, technical and metrical effects. It's a long, difficult job and there can't be any half measures.

I think it's also worth asking people to distinguish between writing things down and being interested in language, because if you're not interested in language and its power of suggestion, you're writing something other than poetry. You don't have to be a linguistic expert, but you do have to be absorbed by the power of language to make the world more real. I suspect the most neglected part of teaching about poetry currently is the sentences in which the poetry emerges. Yet sentence construction is the element over which we have most control in poetry.

I would ask the following questions: Are they consequential? Do they weigh? Do they vary? Are they grammatically vertebrate?

## Who was your favourite poet as a child?

My mother was a headteacher so there were always poetry books at home which she had been given as inspection copies. I loved Lear's '*The Jumblies*', Eliot's '*Old Possum's Book of Practical*

*Cats'* and Browning's '*The Pied Piper of Hamelin*'. They're all very rhythmic and I enjoyed their musical lives, the sense of cadence and turn.

Later, my English teacher, Mr Grayson, introduced me to Eliot's *'Preludes'*, which just blew my head off.

# HANNAH LOWE
# THE REGISTER

*The Register (Early Draft)*

That first September, I climbed the steps, blue-stone
and chipped by a thousand heels, where every hour
the teenage pupils trampled up and down
like a thousand other teenagers before –

the Turkish girls, always hand in hand, the boys
with doodled skateboards under arm. And up
I went, through the stairwell's swarm of bodies, the noise
of first-day-back *salaams*, high fives. At the top

a hall of coloured doors – bright blue, 6B,
my first. Stepped into white sun though the arches,
a horse-shoe of desks, and waiting there for me
on plastic chairs, those kids, those sweet hurt faces.

I called their names – Deniz, Gulay, Danielle –
all back to do what they'd already failed.

## THE PROCESS OF POETRY

### *The Register (Final Version)*

That first September, I climbed the blue stone steps,
past Shakespeare's doubtful face, an old mosaic
of Jamaica, and the ruby blot of lips
where last year's girls had kissed the schoolhouse brick.
Now this year's crop pushed past, all clattery-chat,
their first day back – *Whassup? Salaam!* – the Fugees
blaring from someone's phone: Ready or not...
And with that old white dog still barking softly

in my head, I walked the sugar-papered hall
and pushed the classroom door to find a sprawl
of teenagers sat waiting, my 're-sitters',
all back to do what they'd already failed.
I took my seat, and called the register
Deniz, Tyrone, Alicia, Chantelle –

### How long did it take to write 'The Register' and how many drafts did it go through?

As the poem was meant to be the first one in a sequence, it had to land the reader into the series. I started writing it in 2016 and probably completed it in 2020, so it took around four years. How many drafts? It depends what you count as a new draft. Does changing a word count? If so, I'd say this poem went through around 50 drafts and the version you see here is approximately the twentieth.

People say that the poems in '*The Kids*' are so easy and conversational, which is wonderful, but belies that fact it took forever to write them. Often, I'd lose all sense of time trying to capture the poems as sonnets. I remember, at one stage, I sat on the floor for five hours nonstop fiddling with one of them.

**It's fascinating comparing these two drafts and exploring the different types of changes from the macro to the micro. Can you tell me a little about the form?**

The poems are probably the hardest poems I've written. Originally, I tried to write the sequence as an extended crown, whereby the last line of one poem would become the first line of the next in the sequence. I wrote around 30 poems using that structure and then I realized that it didn't work. However, during the process I was learning about the sonnet form and, most importantly, where the turn, or volta, should go. The turn is really important, moving the reader either spatially, rhetorically or temporally.

As you can see, initially I envisaged the poem as a Shakespearean sonnet with three quatrains and rhyming couplet, but when I reflected more on the turn, it worked better as a Petrarchan sonnet with an octet, followed by a sestet. At first, it was about the physical movement to a different place. Yet, later, I realised the most significant turning point was making clear that I was walking down the corridor on my first day as a teacher.

It's only Petrarchan in relation to the stanza length, not in any other way. The rhyming scheme doesn't conform to the classical Petrarchan sonnet scheme. I've often played hard and loose with the rhyme scheme in the sequence. Aren't rules there to be broken? If it felt important to end with a rhyming couplet for emphasis, I'd use one, even if the rules of the form dictated otherwise.

**On a line-by-line level there are a number of changes, and the language feels much more precise in the final version.**

Yes, you're right. It was initially quite vague in places.

## THE PROCESS OF POETRY

Whenever you have the thought 'I can get away with this', in a poem, you can't. It's taken me years to learn that though. In the first version, *'The noise of first day back salaams'* is in the plural. It was quite generalised and didn't feel direct enough. By making it singular *'Whassup? Salaam!'* I hoped that the effect would be of hearing the students' individual voices, as opposed to my imaginings. The italics and punctuation add to this dynamic of direct speech.

*'The ruby blot of lips'* took a while to work out and I experimented with lots of different coloured blots before settling on *'ruby'*. At one stage they were *'hot pink'*!

*'All clattery-chat, their first day back'* was another addition. The onomatopoeic effect seemed appropriate for the young world in which it is set. Rhyme always excites me and I like the internal rhyme here.

The line *'And with that old white dog still barking softly in my head'* was added at the end of the first stanza because I wanted to carry the white dog image through from the prologue poem, as it symbolises my father's death which was the reason why I became a teacher. In fact, I wish I'd sustained this image in later poems within the collection too.

There's always a teacher's desk, isn't there? It's a useful trope in writing about teaching. When I write *'I took my seat'*, it symbolized my first step inside the classroom and represented the beginning of my teaching career. The desk also symbolises authority and raises questions about my own knowledge and authority in the classroom, ideas which are explored later in the collection.

There were occasional changes in the word order too, so *'steps, blue stone'* becomes *'blue stone steps'* to fit in with the rhyme scheme. The sibilant effect was incidental. I don't really think as much about alliteration. To me, alliteration is often too easily identifiable and perhaps not that sophisticated, although I know other poets might not agree, and certainly there are brilliant uses of this effect in some poems.

## There are a several omissions in the final version, particularly from the earlier third stanza.

Yes, the images in the earlier version didn't feel strong enough in the end and were too vague. A sonnet can only hold so much and, as there are so few words to play with, every single one has to be right. You have to cram as much as you can into a small space, making sure that each image fits with the metre and the rhyme. Constructing a sonnet is also about compromise and working with the line breaks. You want to break the line where it has the most effect, which might be a sense break and might be to delay or draw attention to what comes on the next line.

*'A hall of coloured doors'* becomes *'sugar-papered hall'*, which is more precise. I felt that anyone reading the poem would feel that *'6B'* / *'me'* was only there for the rhyme, so it had to go. Although I liked *'the white sun through the arches'*, I felt it wasn't clear enough as readers might not see the view of the old Victorian school building where I used to teach. The context provided in the opening line, *'That first September'*, shows that this was my first year in teaching and so *'my first'* became redundant and the *'plastic chairs'* were just lazy and only there for the metre.

## Are there any omissions you regret?

I really liked the phrase *'those sweet, hurt faces'*, but unfortunately it didn't make it to the final cut as I just couldn't make it work with the rest of the poem. Much as I wanted it to stay, it had to go.

## *'Deniz, Gulay, Danielle-'* became *'Denis, Tyrone, Alicia, Chantelle-'* in the final draft. How did you go about choosing the names?

Gulay, who is in the earlier version, was a real student of mine, but I never intended to use actual names of students. It was important to me that no real student would be able to recognize themselves.

The names were mainly iambic to fit in with the metre of the poem (they have an unstressed syllable, followed by a stressed syllable) so that was one constraint. Initially, I only needed six syllables worth of names, but because of other alterations, in the final version, I needed ten syllables. In some ways, it was like doing a crossword puzzle or a Sudoku, like trying to solve a puzzle with a metrical beat. There was always a *'Danielle/ Chantelle'* and I chose *'Alicia'* for the metrical feet (2, instead of 1). *'Tyrone* 'was a later addition. I wanted the names to suggest the milieu of students that I had taught, so I was thinking about ethnicity and names – in my head, the names are Turkish, Afro-Caribbean and English.

**I'm interested in your decision to move your initial ending higher and finish, instead, with those names.**

By that point it felt like landing on their names was more important and the focus was on the students themselves, rather than their previous failure. It also offered the names up to the reader as portraits of the students. I wanted there to be a sense of who these characters are. I think it's a more optimistic closing line than *'all back to do what they'd already failed.'*

**Let's talk a little about feedback.**

For over ten years, I attended a writing workshop and used to share my work at that. More recently, during lockdown, I formed a group with poets Richard Scott, Will Harris and Anna Selby and the feedback they provided was incredibly helpful, particularly on the macro level. For example, they would question the tone, or line order, or query what was missing from a piece. They would suggest changes and my gut instinct would be no, as it won't work with the metre and rhythm. But then I'd often see they were right, and I would work to reorder the poem in response to their suggestions.

After almost twenty years of writing and many courses on poetry, sometimes back-to-back, I don't feel that I require feedback as much. I've always really needed it, but now, I can usually see the problems in my own poems. Despite this, if I were putting a new manuscript together, I would want to share again. Even if I think a poem is finished, there's always something I won't have thought of.

## Do you have a writing routine?

I have commissions and deadlines, so that provides an impetus. However, that's as far as my 'writing routine' goes. I have a young son, a job, a social life and sometimes it feels that life is overfull with competing activities. But I do find time for writing. Last night, just as I was going to bed, I spent twenty minutes tweaking a poem.

## What do you find easiest about writing a poem?

I love form and would always choose it over free verse. To me, free verse is like diving into an ocean, whereas form is like diving into a swimming pool with lanes and lifeguards and safe boundaries.

I really enjoy playing around with rhyme and meter to find the rhythm. It's like doing a Rubik's Cube, trying different combinations to find the best fit. I think my understanding of rhythm comes from playing the piano, and that understanding musical elements like time signatures has been enormously beneficial for working with rhythm in poetry. Some people don't have as clear a sense of rhythm and might find they are more drawn to free verse. But free verse also needs music and cadence.

## Conversely, what is your biggest challenge when writing?

I think my vocabulary and syntax aren't that exciting in free verse, but when you're writing a sonnet, every word must be the right word, in the right place. I like to push at language and syntax by using expressions that aren't in my lexicon. I use a rhyming dictionary and thesaurus to help me to find exciting and dynamic word choices.

Although it's a challenge, I enjoy the rethinking and revisioning, and feel so pleased when I think I poem is 'there', as in finished.

**After fifty drafts, how did you know that the poem was finished?**

I probably felt I'd nailed it. The rhymes and the metre finally worked. Normally, when I have that feeling, there's not much that needs changing, it's more a case of fine tuning, maybe altering one word or the punctuation or graphology.

**What advice do you have for aspiring poets?**

You can't write well without doing the work. Maybe you have talent, but talent is nothing without slog! No published writer has succeeded without putting an extraordinary amount of effort into their writing. The first draft is the least of your problems!

# REGI CLAIRE
# (UN)CERTAINTIES – AN EXTRACT

## *(Un)certainties: An Extract (Early Draft)*

True or false – please tick as appropriate

My sister loved
A. her family
B. her partner
C. kayaks

My sister's partner loved
A. her
B. his family
C. kayaks

My sister sent her children
A. a WhatsApp text saying she was excited about that day's 10km kayaking trip with her partner
B. a picture of the mirror-smooth sea
C. a selfie in a swim vest
D. emojis of dolphins

My sister's postcard to our parents
A. was sent before the kayaking trip
B. was sent by hotel staff after the kayaking trip
C. arrived ten days after the kayaking trip

# THE PROCESS OF POETRY

My sister died
A. on Friday 13th
B. on Saturday 14th

My sister's partner did not die
A. on Friday 13th
B. on Saturday 14th

My sister died alone
A. soon after sunset in a storm at sea
B. in the dark in a storm at sea
C. in the hours of dawn after a storm at sea
D. in sunlight on the morning after a storm at sea

My sister's partner clung to his kayak alone
A. from sunset to dawn in a storm at sea
B. from sunset to sunrise in a storm at sea and the calmness beyond
C. from sunset to sunlit morning in a storm at sea and the calmness beyond

My sister died because
A. she and her partner spent time on various beaches, picnicking, shell-gathering, sunbathing, resting
B. she and her partner spent time exploring the disused submarine base inside the cliffs near the promontory
C. she was afraid of the dark inside the submarine base and so she sang, seated in her kayak as her partner listened, sang her heart out for the soaring echo of it, and the echo could not bear to lose her and her voice

My sister died because
A. the mirror smoothness of the water began to break and broken mirrors always signify misfortune
B. the waves were too small at first to seem alarming
C. the waves grew in strength slowly

## *(Un)certainties: An Extract (Final Version)*

My sister once gave me
A. an ultramarine silk scarf
B. a star-shaped candlestick of clear glass
C. a guardian angel made from clay and driftwood

My sister loved
A. her family
B. her partner
C. kayaks

My sister's partner loved
A. her
B. his family
C. kayaks

My sister and her partner loved
A. adventure
B. sports
C. water
D. the sea

My sister and her partner
A. had been on sea kayaking trips before
B. were familiar with that coastline
C. were offered a guided tour
D. trusted their abilities and experience

My sister sent her children
A. a WhatsApp message saying how excited she was about that day's 10 km kayaking trip
B. a picture of the mirror-smooth sea
C. a selfie in a swim vest
D. emojis of dolphins

## THE PROCESS OF POETRY

My sister's postcard to our parents
A. was sent before the kayaking trip
B. was sent by hotel staff after the kayaking trip
C. arrived ten days after the kayaking trip, before her funeral

My sister died
A. on Friday 13th
B. on Saturday 14th

My sister's partner did not die
A. on Friday 13th
B. on Saturday 14th

My sister died at sea, alone
A. soon after sunset in a storm
B. in the dark in a storm
C. at dawn, after a storm
D. in sunlight, on the morning after a storm

My sister's partner clung to his kayak at sea, alone
A. from sunset to false dawn throughout a storm
B. from sunset to sunrise throughout a storm and the calm hours beyond
C. from sunset to sunlit morning throughout a storm and the calm hours beyond

My sister died because
A. she and her partner spent time on a series of beaches along the coast, picnicking, shell-gathering, sunbathing, resting
B. she and her partner spent time exploring the disused submarine tunnel under the cliffs
C. she was afraid of the dark inside the tunnel and so she sang, seated in her kayak as her partner listened, sang her heart out for the soaring echo of it, and the echo could not bear to lose her and her voice

My sister died because

A. the mirror smoothness of the water began to break, and broken mirrors bring bad luck
B. the waves were too small to seem alarming
C. the waves grew in strength only slowly

## Can you tell us a little about the origins of the poem?

In mid-March 2019 I woke up one morning and just knew that unless I wrote about my sister's recent death in a kayaking accident, my grief would completely overwhelm and silence me. I wondered how to go about it. I felt I needed some kind of logical format to avoid sounding overwrought or melodramatic.

At the time I was a fiction writer and simply considered '(Un)certainties' a short story, even sent it out as such. But after a close friend read the text and kept calling it 'your poem', I began to reconsider and finally submitted it to *Mslexia* magazine's poetry competition.

## How long did it take to write the poem?

Only about three weeks. I worked on it most days, feeling quite driven, and finished it in early April 2019. Parts of it I first 'wrote' in my head during a dog walk. The earlier drafts grew more or less organically; the later ones involved just a few tweaks, like shifting a stanza or changing a word or two. There were never any radical rewrites. The poem went through around 13 actual drafts and the one you have here is the fifth.

## The multiple-choice framework is a fascinating device. How did this arise?

It came to me suddenly, like an epiphany, as I lay in bed that March morning. The form seemed perfect for a narrative that mixed fact with fiction, allowing me to list the certainties and the many unanswered questions about my sister's death, and thus to chronicle my distress. When I mentioned the idea to my husband, he said, 'Well, it might work. It'll depend on what you do with it.'

**As we compare the two versions of the poem, there are different types of changes including a new stanza, a change in the order of the existing stanzas, alterations to the vocabulary and indeed to some of the punctuation. What do you see as the biggest change as the work developed?**

The first version was only a page long and rather 'in-your-face'. As the poem developed, it became longer, clearer and took on a more narrative dimension. Because the loss impacted on my whole family, I brought in my sister's children and our parents in later drafts. I agonised over how to include my brother, but in the end, just couldn't see a way.

A crucial addition was the phrase '*before her funeral*' in the sixth stanza. It jolts the reader and functions like a narrative gear change.

**There is a new stanza at the very beginning. What does this bring to the poem as a whole?**

Perhaps ironically, the first stanza was one of the very last parts of the poem to be written. It didn't appear at all until the seventh version. As the multiple-choice format made the poem sound quite staccato, I felt the reader needed a gentler lead-in.

I also wanted to 'frame' the poem and contextualise it more. Although I appeared as a character in the final stanza, it seemed important to present myself as such from the outset, to emphasise the actual, personal relationship between my sister and me, not merely our genetic link. The early drafts didn't do this. By introducing myself as the recipient of her gifts, I became a real character and our relationship one of love, kindness and generosity.

My sister gave me many presents over her lifetime, and the first stanza is based on an unconscious selection of those items.

The *'ultramarine silk scarf'* serves as an image of the sea in which she died and also works alliteratively, along with *'star'*, which in turn evokes the idea of a guiding light or a *'guardian angel'*. I am very conscious that she herself didn't have a guardian angel. I thought hard about what word to use for 'blue', toying with many synonyms, including 'indigo', but when I found *'ultramarine'* with its etymology of 'beyond the sea', it felt exactly right.

The choice of materials was significant too. The *'glass'* because of its fragility, the *'clay'* as both a reminder of the mud my sister and I played in as children and the earth we go back to in death, suggesting both our origins as humans and our inherent mortality.

I think that, ultimately, this first stanza encapsulates the whole poem. It foreshadows what is to come by setting up thematic, figurative and narrative strands.

### Did this first stanza alter significantly as the poem developed?

Once it was written, the stanza changed very little. B. initially read *'a star-shaped candlestick of clear glass with wave patterns'*. I cut *'wave patterns'* in version 8 as the line was too much of a mouthful and the reference to *'wave'* too blatant (even though that particular candlestick from my sister does have a wave pattern on its underside…). Everything else matches the final version.

### In the final version some stanzas were given greater prominence.

Yes, having written a 'complete' draft, I was able to step back and see that some of the stanzas near the end clearly belonged at the beginning. I'd written them down as they came to me, without much thought of the narrative. Later, like pieces in a jigsaw, they had to be slotted into their rightful place, as was the case with the fourth and fifth stanzas.

## Let's turn to some of the vocabulary changes.

Some words took a lot of working out, like *'ultramarine'*. In the eleventh stanza, I originally used the phrase *'in a storm'*. But *'in'* didn't give a sense of duration, unlike *'throughout'*. I felt that *'calmness'* wasn't strong enough, whereas *'calm hours'*, with its two equal stresses, helped emphasise the surreal sense of tranquility and sounded more elegiac.

The next stanza contains several changes, partly inspired by my research into the area where my sister had died. I used Google Maps to try and pinpoint the location. I replaced *'various beaches'* with *'a series of beaches'* to reflect the progressive nature of the trip and to add assonance – the keening *'i'* slows the line down and increases the threat of the storm. For accuracy, *'base'* became *'tunnel'*. The preposition *'under'* in *'under the cliffs'* sounded more menacing than *'inside'* and there's the added assonance of the *'u'* in *'submarine'*, *'tunnel'* and *'under'* (also, I wanted rid of the repetition of *'inside'*). Similarly, *'the dark inside the tunnel'* felt more claustrophobic than *'the dark inside the submarine base'*.

## Is there any part of this early draft with which you were particularly unhappy?

Yes, absolutely. In stanza thirteen, the phrase *'always signify misfortune'* now makes me cringe. Sometimes simpler words work better than a more complex vocabulary. The polysyllabic *'signify'* is Latinate and completely the wrong register, so it became *'bring'*; *'misfortune'*, also Latinate and polysyllabic, became *'bad luck'*. I cut the superfluous *'always'* and ended up with three monosyllables: *'bring bad luck'*, all requiring equal stress, with the *'k'* of *'luck'* adding extra harshness and emphasis (the feminine ending of *'misfortune'* felt too weak).

## I notice in the tenth stanza you change the positioning of *'at sea'* which initially appears at the end of each line?

I realised that *'at sea'* was a common denominator and therefore belonged in the introductory line rather than the multiple-choice options.

**You also made a slight alteration to the punctuation in this stanza.**

Yes, it felt important to add a comma in *'My sister died at sea, alone'* in order to emphasise her utter isolation and let the reader pause. I did the same in the introductory line of the next stanza, about her partner: *'My sister's partner clung to his kayak at sea, alone.'* The parallelism highlights their separate aloneness.

The commas in the options of the tenth stanza took me some time to decide on. I wondered if a comma was required after *'in the dark'*, putting it in then cutting it again. Commas did feel necessary, however, after *'at dawn'* and *'in sunlight'*, for added gravitas.

**Did it always have this title?**

Not at all. The titles kept changing. There were variants on *'True or False'* (version 1). For example, *'True or false – please tick as appropriate'* (versions 2-6) and *'True or false – please choose to the best of your understanding'* (version 7). While these issued an imperative, *'choose'*, and therefore involved the reader, I soon realised they didn't work in other ways. Ultimately, they felt perfunctory and inappropriate, cheapening the tragedy. The titles of the eighth and ninth versions were *'Guesswork'* and *'You make your own story'* respectively, and equally unsatisfactory.

'(Un)certainties' (version 10 onwards) felt absolutely right. The use of parenthesis allowed me to contrast, and yet bridge, fact and conjecture. The very form of the title seemed to reflect its meaning, as if certainties and uncertainties were entwined. I hoped that the title's abstract nature would provide a rational counterpoint to a poem imbued with emotion, saving it from melodrama.

## Can we talk a little about your working methods? Do you have a particular routine?

No, I don't really have a routine or plan. Once or twice I've 'written' whole poems in my head. Occasionally, fragments of short stories have become poems.

I started out as a short story writer and used to take ages thinking about sound, rhythm and imagery besides the narrative. 'You work like a poet,' my husband always said. And yes, my scrupulous slowness has proved a boon for my poetry.

I like working at night. Often, I lie in bed thinking of lines, ideas, associations. These are fleeting and, unless written down, unrecoverable. I remember once waking up very early and, not wanting to disturb my husband, grabbing a pen and a tissue to jot down some stanzas I knew I'd otherwise forget. When I ran out of tissue, I used a bookmark to continue my notes as I couldn't bring myself to deface the book itself.

## How do you know when a poem is truly finished?

That's a good question. The short answer is you don't. With '(Un)certainties', for instance, I spent quite a bit of time trying to include my brother and add more details. However, I was mindful that too much might weaken the impact and lose the reader.

Yet, even now I sometimes think that I would like to expand it as there is more to tell.

## Do you have any writing tips for beginners?

Read and read and read. Try to write what only you can write. I believe that poems often come from a more personal part of ourselves than other types of writing; there must be some personal core, otherwise why bother writing them at all? I suspect that '(Un)certainties' resonated with so many people because we all experience grief in one way or another.

I think it's important to open yourself up to feedback. Perhaps not at the very beginning though, as this can be discouraging.

## THE PROCESS OF POETRY

What you write isn't going to be perfect straightaway. Free write, then chisel away and find out what it's about. Sometimes a poem begins with an extended central metaphor or image. What's the key image or idea in your poem? I am a great believer in editing. Sensitive, occasionally ruthless, editing will make your writing sing.

# GILLIAN CLARKE

# THE PIANO

*The Piano (Early Draft)*

THE PROCESS OF POETRY

## *The Piano (Final Version)*

The last bus sighs through the stops of the sleeping suburb
and he's home again with a click of keys, a step on the stairs.
I see him again, shut in the upstairs sitting-room
in that huge Oxfam overcoat, one hand shuffling
through the music, the other lifting the black wing.

My light's out in the room he was born in. In the hall
the clock clears its throat and counts twelve hours
into space. His scales rise, falter and fall back –
not easy to fly on one wing, even for him
with those two extra digits he was born with.

I should have known there'd be music as he flew, singing,
and the midwife cried out, 'Magic fingers!' A small variation,
born with more, like obsession. They soon fell,
tied like the cord, leaving a small scar fading
on each hand like a memory of flight.

Midnight arpeggios, Bartok, Schubert. I remember,
kept in after school, the lonely sound of a piano lesson
through an open window between-times, sun on the lawn
and everyone gone, the piece played over and over
to the metronome of tennis. Sometimes in the small hours,

after two, the hour of his birth, I lose myself listening
to that little piece by Schubert, perfected in the darkness
of space where the stars are so bright they cast shadows,
and I wait for that waterfall of notes,
as if two hands were not, enough.

## Can we explore the origins of the poem?

As you can see from my notebook, this poem actually began whilst I was tutoring a workshop at the Writer's Centre, Ty Newydd. It was in response to a writing exercise that I set for the students. If you look at the top of the page you can see that the task was to choose a setting, a character and a significant object. I did this at the same time as my students and then we shared our work. My subject was my son, Owain, who was playing the piano after coming home late one night.

## How many drafts did you write and over how long?

I wrote the first draft of the poem in long hand as I always do. I don't really do drafts; I just scribble a few ideas down and tweak the odd word. There were three drafts before the final piece.

Don't forget that although the end of the process may be quick, an intense piece of writing is preceded by many months of germination, thinking and exploring the idea in my head whilst doing something completely mundane. Although I might be thinking about several poems over some months, in a day, or an evening, or a falling asleep hour, there would only be one poem in my mind at once.

## How important is truth in poetry?

The truth is crucial. I never tell lies in poems, never. I don't use false description to get a line. It won't convince if it isn't real and what's the point of not making it authentic?

Any poem must come out of your own experience. You can be connected to, and fired up by, what you see of the world, but you can't put in false things. We all know all of the emotions and those are the things that you use.

For this particular poem we were living in Cardiff just a few hundred yards from the bus stop and I often listened for my son, Owain, to come home from the last bus, thinking if he isn't on that, where is he? He must have been about sixteen or seventeen. 'In that huge Oxfam overcoat' is exactly how he used to dress; I'm not making it up. There was a lot of music when my children were growing up and we had a baby grand piano which Owain played when he came home late at night. He was born with two extra tiny digits and the midwife did, indeed, make the comment about his musicality.

Similarly, 'Miracle on St David's Day' is completely based on a true story. I was invited to go and read to residents at an institution in Abergavenny. There was a huge man standing in the corner who hadn't spoken for many years, yet my poetry sparked something in his memory and the moment happened exactly as I have described it.

## How did family life impact on your work?

I know that some poets find it challenging juggling family life with their work, but it's family life that got my words going and my children were my inspiration. The first poem that I had published was 'Sundial', which I wrote when my son was six. He was playing outside in the garden and I was sunbathing and watching him as he made a clock on the grass. Then I went inside and wrote this on a piece of paper. It was that simple. As I didn't go out to work, I was there for my children and read stories and nursery rhymes to them. They wrote things and I wrote things. Family life enabled my writing to flourish and in many respects my poetry is a journal of my life.

## Lived experience seems to play a strong role in your work.

Yes, absolutely everything I write is either lived experience or distant experience. I don't ever write fiction. Something triggers in the moment and then you have the memories of a lifetime from which to form a response. For me, it's a way of being which started when I was little.

The way I want writers to work is to go into themselves, into their memories, to scribble, and more memory will come. We all have decades and decades of things we've seen, things we've heard and other sensory experiences, so we don't have to make those things up, they're already there inside us. In that first moment when you're writing, the real is in that accumulated experience as well as in the present moment.

Whilst I tend to focus on my own experiences, I also write about events happening elsewhere. I live on a secluded smallholding in the Welsh countryside, but thanks to BBC Radio 4 and The Guardian, the world is very close, and I feel highly attuned to it, perhaps even more so than if I were in a more populous area.

## How do you make commissioned poems resonate with your own experience?

I've written many commissioned poems in my life. When I wrote 'Six Bells' for the fiftieth anniversary of the forty-four miners killed in the mining disaster there, it related to a very different community, but I sought to find a connection. *'Perhaps a woman hanging out the wash paused,'* hopefully, gives me a place to begin.

## You have spoken of poetry as 'word music'. Can you elucidate?

Yes, I would describe poetry as word music because the way that I have learnt poetry is through the sounds. To me, poetry is an instinct, I don't have a method. I'm not thinking of musicality, I'm hearing it and that's an important distinction for me. It is all about listening. I feel that I'm a singer, more than a writer. Poetry is a rhythmic way of thinking. I don't think and count and put in metaphors, for me it's a telling.

Once I have captured the first ideas and phrases on the page, I say it out loud. I then type what I 'hear', but it shapes as I type, so that I see, as well as hear, it. Lines shape sound, as we know. What goes on the page has to help the reader to hear what you have heard, by setting it out in its bars.

## Do you think about poetry when you're not actively writing it?

It's in my mind a great deal of the time. It's so instinctive to me that I can't count without using a counting rhyme. Whatever

I'm doing, whether I'm preparing food or pruning flowers or trying to tidy up, I have rhymes in my head.

## Do you ever find it hard to complete a poem?

It's rare for me to have trouble completing a poem, but there's a poem in my current manuscript with which I am having tremendous difficulty as I want it to be perfect, and it isn't. Yesterday a sonnet line came to me and I wonder if that's where I'm going. Because of my love of Shakespeare, I do like iambic pentameters, but I don't know how it will end up. I've written many sonnets, but they're not highly formal.

## As one of the founders of the Writers' Centre, Ty Newydd, what is your advice for emerging poets?

I don't think you can teach a non- poet to write poetry from scratch, but I think you can persuade anybody to find inside themselves a language to express something that's deeply true to them. I always encourage students to make sure that they can see, hear and really feel the experience.

I want the poet's own voice to be the decider. Read and listen before you scribble anything down. I'd love it if nobody had a paper and pen for a whole day and explored what they could hear in their heads.

Precision with language is vital. Often I look at a poem and it seems cluttered with an excessive use of adverbs and adjectives. Think of Yeats' phrase in 'The Second Coming', 'Slouches towards Bethlehem'. He doesn't say, 'walks clumsily', does he? Choose the right word and you won't need to embellish it. Write clearly and then give it a shock.

Furthermore, the shape mustn't take over from the sound. I want to put on the page something that you can hear.

Reading and learning and saying poetry is for everybody, as is using diaries and journals to record one's feelings, but not everybody should be a poet. I write a journal every day. I'm now on my fifty-eighth. My advice would be just to write poetry, but don't have it as an ambition.

Finally, don't be put off if you really want to do it. Whilst my English teacher, Kathleen Tierney, encouraged me and said she thought that I could be a writer, when I wrote something at Cardiff University, my professor told me that I should forget about it and focus on my studies.

## You have translated poetry from Welsh to English. What are the challenges of translating such a precise form of language?

'The Gododdin' is the earliest series of poems in the British Isles, long before 'Beowulf'. It contains a hundred laments on the deaths of soldiers from a battle long ago. There are two or three academic translations which are not poetic and I thought it was time that someone captured the poetry, without losing the meaning. I wanted to make it worth reading in English.

The Welsh language is incredibly difficult. If you translate French, you're following a familiar pattern with the sentence structure, but here it can be a completely different construction. It wasn't written down so you would need rhyme to ensure that people could remember it. I've maintained the sense of rhymes, but I've had to move the meaning around to get it. All you can do is your best.

## Can we talk about arranging a collection?

If you're a writer and you keep writing about something, you suddenly realise that you have an obsession. Then, when you are working on a collection, there is a worry that you might have too much material on the same narrow topic.

Ordering the poems within a collection can be helped if you have some sort of framework. During lockdown, I suddenly realised that for the first time we didn't know what time, or even day, it was. I based my current collection, *'The Silence'*, around the times of the day nones, vespers and so on which provided a clear structure within which to assemble the poems.

## What impact did poetry have on you as a child? Will today's children have the same experience?

There are three areas from which I learnt so much: nursery rhymes, skipping games and Shakespeare. All of these provided an important aural experience.

From the first nursery rhyme I heard, I've always gravitated towards poetry. Nursery rhymes in the English language are great literature and there isn't another culture that has anything quite like it. They are so important for small children.

I think that the school environment is less conducive to nurturing poetry than in my day. It's a disaster for literature that children are no longer engaging in playground games. I feel it's also important for schools to encourage students to stand up and recite poems from the earliest age.

I have never read a play by Shakespeare on the page, though I know many lines and speeches by heart. They are part of me, and their music influences my writing. My Aunt Phyllis took me to all new productions at Stratford-Upon-Avon until I was twenty-one. The first was King Lear, when I was ten years old. She may have wondered how much I understood, but it was all too real to me. I knew about father-daughter troubles, and my heart was with both Lear and Cordelia.

# ALL THE MEN I NEVER MARRIED NO.42
# KIM MOORE

*All the Men I Never Married No.42 (Early Draft)*

> really" I said as —
>
> Is it — if it's your husband/boyfriend/friend
> is it — if you are arguing, и he spits
> in your face, и to stop the argument
> you open your legs, is it — if you don't
> say no, is it — if you can't say the
> word, is it — if afterwards you pretend
> it never happened, is it — if you don't
> struggle, if you become still as water
> ~~in~~ in November, if you become grey
> if something inside you, some bright pool
> of desire, goes into hiding for years,
> is it — if she can't say the word,
> if she can't meet your eye, when she
> tells you, is it — if he didn't do it to
> you, if she can't remember, is it —

## THE PROCESS OF POETRY

### *All the Men I Never Married No.42 (Final Version)*

Is it ▓ if your husband/boyfriend/friend did it, is it ▓ if you didn't say no/yes, if you were arguing/not speaking, is it ▓ if he spits in your face and you just want it to stop, is it ▓ if you can't even write it, is it ▓ if you can't even say it, if you opened your legs, if you didn't protest, if you stayed with him after, is it ▓ if you pretend nothing has happened, is it ▓ if you did it to distract him, to make him stop shouting, to make him stop swearing, to make him stop leaving, is it ▓ if you became grey, if some bright fish of desire went into hiding for years, is it ▓ if you were frightened, not for your life, but for your mind, is it ▓ if your mind was slipping away and doing it was the only thing that stopped the slipping, is it ▓ if you did it so you could sleep, is it ▓ if you did it to stand in for forgiveness, if you had hate in your heart when you did it, if you had lies in your chest, is it ▓ if you didn't mean it, if you can't remember what happened, is it still ▓ if you never told anyone, if you didn't think about it again, if you moved on, if you're ok now, if you're ok now, if you're ok now.

## Can you tell me a little about the origins of the poem?

This is a very personal poem which I have never discussed or read in public. It arose from a conversation with a friend. Through that conversation, I started to question an experience which had happened to me and whether my recollection of it was accurate. The poem raises so many caveats which, I think, is what women do in this situation. I've spoken to many people with similar stories who have responded in this way.

## How did this translate into the poem?

I noticed that throughout the initial conversation we both avoided articulating the word. Although I'd been writing about gender-based violence as part of my PhD, I was still very uncomfortable talking about it. I find it hard to say the word even now. The whole poem revolves around not talking about rape, despite the fact that it was at the very heart of the conversation, and having the word blacked out is a visual representation of this erasure. It was never spoken or written at all. Even in the first draft, it wasn't written, there were just little zigzags underneath the scribble.

At first, when you asked me to discuss this poem my immediate reaction was no, not that one, but then I thought that it could be interesting to talk about it as a creative process, and that maybe that discomfort in itself is worth exploring.

## I completely understand the need to erase the word, but did you ever consider using other means?

I considered using just a blank space, but that seemed a more passive approach and failed to accurately convey the violent nature of this act. If it was just a white space, it would seem as if the silence had taken over from the word, which in a way mirrors the problem, a key part of which is that conversations about rape are silenced. It was very important to me to have the blacked-out boxes in the poem. The black square is an action and my decision to cover up the word affords me a sense of control. I regard it as a political poem.

## Let's explore the redrafting process.

This was a relatively short process as the versions are quite similar, so there were probably around twenty rewrites, although some of those may have minor tweaks. I often get most of the body of the poem and then rewrite it over and over again and make quite tiny changes. I always begin writing in long hand in my notebook and then, after a few drafts, some pieces make it on to my laptop where I develop them further. Looking at my notebook, I can see that I started writing some other poems in between, but they didn't develop, and then I've gone back to that one and it's grown a lot longer. I probably left it alone for around a month to 'cook' in my notebook.

As I hand write first drafts, my notebook is full of lengthy chunks of prose, so looking at them, you wouldn't know that I was a poet. When I return to them, it feels as if they've been written by someone else, which gives me a little bit of distance. That's when I would put the line breaks in or, in this case, realise that it was a prose poem.

## I'm interested in your decision to change the tense from the present to the past.

In the first draft, I was writing in the moment after the conversation and didn't realise that I was writing about myself. By the final version, I realised that it was about something set in my past, so felt the change of tense was necessary.

## Did this awareness lead to your change of subject too?

Yes, the first draft is very visceral. In the final published version, the *'she'* disappears. In the first draft, because I use *'she'* and then flip to *'you'*, I feel I'm losing control of the pronouns. The *'she'* became a distraction because as the poem developed it became less about my friend's experience and more about my own. I am talking to myself, yet I'm also addressing the reader.

**It is interesting to see the changes to the opening line of the poem.**

I repositioned the words '*if you didn't say no*' from the fourth to the opening line, as I wanted to make them more visible, rather than burying it in the poem. After a few drafts, I realised that this particular line, which raises the question of consent, needed more prominence. I didn't place it at the beginning of the line as the first question is who is doing this to you and does the type of relationship offer any excuse. This poem is really exploring internal misogyny, because it was only in the writing of these questions that I could answer myself and think, well no, of course these caveats don't excuse rape!

As I had been writing quickly, when I read it back, I realised that it didn't make sense without the addition of '*did it*'. Without these words there was no specific action. I also wanted to keep repeating '*it*'.

**Tell me about your use of alternatives.**

Partly these were about clarity, but they were also about all of the caveats that might be raised. So, in the final draft I feel like I'm trying to get this sense of uncertainty. Consent should not be this immovable, fixed thing – consent can be given and then withdrawn at any time – it should be an active process that both partners are engaged in.

What happens if we don't remember if we said no? What happens if we can't remember if we said yes? How can we find language for those difficult experiences? Similarly, with '*arguing/not speaking*' I added '*not speaking*', as I wanted to explore the different ways that we resist. We resist in the way that we feel keeps us safest, and our silence can be used against us.

At one point, I experimented with forward slashes instead of commas, but combined with the blackness it felt too cluttered.

## There are some other additions and alterations.

Yes, *'And to stop the argument'* becomes *'And you just want it to stop'* which places *'you'* at the centre and is far more active and direct.

*'No'* becomes *'protest'* for a number of reasons. First, I'd already used *'no'* earlier within the poem, secondly *'no'* is a tiny word and *'protest'* is a more active, stronger word. Finally, *'protest'* works better sonically with *'open'* in the previous clause and with the overall rhythm.

## There is less imagery in the final version.

Your brain starts to reach for a poem rather than letting it happen. I remember writing the line *'still water in November'*. Until that moment, I didn't know if this piece of writing was just an outlet for my feelings. When I reached that point, I realised that my brain wanted to write a poem, but it's such a fine balancing and that was too self-consciously poetic and also lacking in originality. These are all split second decisions.

Then the fish image arose, and the fish coming into sight and hiding again is where it felt like it would either turn into a poem or fall apart. When I'm writing a poem, I sometimes push it to ridiculous limits to see what is possible, and this was the risk point.

I removed *'if something inside you'* because it was implicit that the fish of desire was inside you, which made this phrase redundant.

## What led to the change in ending?

I wanted to write about resistance, but the poem is also exploring female guilt and complicity. Importantly, I didn't want to end on the word 'rape'. Putting it at the end of the poem would have given it a power and prominence that I wasn't prepared to give it.

It's addressing me, and other women, who excuse sexual assaults and challenging the pretence that we have not been seriously affected by them. The minimisation of a traumatic event is also a kind of coping mechanism in order to deal with what has happened. The repetition could be viewed as a comfort, but why would you need to repeat it if you really are okay?

## Let's talk a little about the punctuation.

Whilst some of the vocabulary changed, one thing that didn't change throughout all of the drafts was the single sentence. Whereas some poems are written slowly, I remember writing this in a big rush and throughout all of the drafts, I realised I wanted to maintain the energy and the stream of consciousness effect.

## This appears in your collection *All the Men I Never Married*. What was the impetus for this?

I began writing the poems for the collection in 2016 and it was directly related to my PhD researching misogyny and gender-based violence. During this period, I saw Claudia Rankine read '*Citizen*', which was transformational and made me think about my complicity in racist structures. I had the lofty ambition that I could change people's attitudes by writing poems about sexism, in the same way that Claudia Rankine was writing about, and influencing people's perceptions of, racism.

I was keen to focus on lyric poetry and try to explore what happened if you put the white space of a poem around an experience. What I found was that it made it impossible for me to minimise or dismiss the experiences of sexism, and I hope it creates points of conversation and reflection for readers. The inherent qualities of lyric poetry, and the white space, highlighted these experiences and made them impossible to ignore.

## How did you first get interested in poetry?

I stole a poetry anthology from school. I've still got it on my bookshelf, and I ought to take it back one day. I really loved Tennyson and learnt some of his poems, like 'Tithonus', off by heart. Later, when I went to university to study music, I used to pop into Borders in Leeds every couple of weeks and buy a poetry book by Billy Collins, Charles Bukowski or Carol Ann Duffy.

## You are the mother of a young child, how does this fit in with a writing routine?

It doesn't! I don't have any sort of routine because my day is governed by the rhythm of everything else that's going on in my life. I used to worry about not writing any more poems, but I never worry about that now.

A writing routine doesn't merely involve writing poems, it also involves reading them. I'm just beginning to read again, and I'll read for the next six months before I even start writing any more poems. I feel that I need to read more, otherwise I'll just be repeating myself.

That's not completely true; I have started writing a few poems about motherhood that I keep in a new poems document, but I'm in a state of denial about it. I've got seventy-five pages in it now.

## As a creative writing lecturer, what advice do you give to your students?

My main advice would be to find and read poets who are creating something similar to the work you are aiming to produce, and start to develop your thinking around the themes you are interested in. Before writing this collection, I read Maggie Nelson's *'Bluets',* which is a kind of cross between prose and poetry. The way she concentrates on the colour blue and considers it from different angles is kind of what I've done in 'All the Men I Never Married', but focusing on sexism and female desire instead.

Since finishing my PhD, I'm a big believer in honouring your own creative process – so first of all finding out what makes you write, how your mind works, and then leaning into it and celebrating it. I spent so much time comparing the way I worked to the way other people worked and feeling that I wasn't getting it 'right'. It was only when I finally realised there is no right way that things started to fall into place. If my brain wants to leap from film theory to feminism to close reading to philosophy, then I have to go with it, and enjoy the ride.

# CAROLINE BIRD
# THE FINAL EPISODE

*Unnamed journal entry*

Will you forgive me in advance?
I'm not going to be like the other mums, baby,
To be honest I'm not even going to try.
They'll be loads of things I'll be supposed to care about
That I won't care about. I'll forget forms.
What will the limits of your tolerance be?
How much strangeness will you tolerate?
Will you tolerate me? Can I be me?
Will you take me as I am? Could I do a piece
Of naked televised performance art?
If I thoroughly explained the artistic merit?
Would you let me be a stripper? Do porn?
Or would you resent me, judge me, feel neglected?
Can I flip out now and then so long as I never hurt you?
Can I, once, punch a pillow and scream and slightly scare you?
If I explain afterwards? I'll never push you down the stairs
Like my dad did by accident. Can I disappear for a month
When you're thirteen and then return? What reasonable
Fuck ups with you permit? Can I run out of money
One Christmas and just get you stuff from charity shops?
Can I get really tired and snap at you? Then apologise?
Can I, once, close a door in your face and say 'not now.'

# THE PROCESS OF POETRY

If I feel ashamed straight after and never do it again?
Can I fall in love with someone who isn't your mother?
Would you understand that? Or would your hatred
Of me increase exponentially with every tear
That dropped down her face? Even if you knew it was a pattern
Of mine, even if I explained and explained?
When Joni Mitchell sang to California asking 'will you take
Me as I am, strung out on another man,' what did
California reply? Will you be my California?
Will you take me as I am? Strung out on another woman?
If I never abandon you? If I love you forever?
I don't wanna be grovelling in the foetal position
In a group therapy room when I'm seventy five
Like my daddy did. I don't wanna have to apologise
And apologise for the nature of my character.
If I try my best? How much of my character
Will you interpret as flawed? Will I make you feel safe?
Will you let me?

# THE PROCESS OF POETRY

## *The Final Episode (Final Version)*

The 18$^{th}$ century bawd who sells her daughter's virginity
to an Earl. The tired CIA operative who says "just do it"
then half a village dies. The plantation owner's wife.
The lonely CEO of the pharmaceutical company
who screams like a banshee when an employee's baby
pukes milk on her pant-suit. The detective who clicks
her zippo underneath the incriminating photo of her boss.
The 'complex' one who lets her servant girl be whipped.
Who dumps the radioactive material in the reservoir.
Who is given a chance to apologise to a crying friend
and instead pauses and says "fuck off." Who is unable
to report her violent husband before he murders someone.
Unable to stop the drone pilot from pressing the button.
Scared of losing her promotion. Covers her ears. Utters
lines like "I believe you are mistaken, my dear" and
"This is above your pay-grade, kid, keep your nose out."
Who says "Fine! Fucking fine!" when the partner who
loves her but can't live like this anymore says "I love you
but I can't live like this anymore." Who thinks the truth
would spoil everything. Who burns the crucial letter.
Whose cleavage is angry and heaving. Who drinks
miniature vodkas in the hotel bath and nearly drowns.
Who wears her new husband's dead ex wife's earrings
to the christening. Who can't forgive her step-son
for existing. Who lets the suicide call go to voicemail.
Who walks to the AA meeting, is met at the church gate
by the greeter who says "welcome" to which she replies

"fuck you creep" and keeps on walking. Who is sick
in the sink. Who suddenly feels the weight of her actions.
Who hyperventilates into a paper bag. Who splashes water
on her face in a public bathroom, glares at the mirror
and says "Wise up." Who knows her narrative arc is peaking,
knows there's goodness in her somewhere, the viewers
have glimpsed it in close-ups and now they're halfway
through the final episode and she's got twenty-two minutes
to wrangle a denouement, fall on her dagger, hand over
the list, clear her spiritual debt in a single payment. Look
at her standing on your porch-step, holding out her heart
like an injured bird and begging you to ruin her.

## Where did the concept for 'The Final Episode' originate?

This poem was very unusual in that it didn't even begin as a poem. What you see here is simply a jotting in my journal, as I tried to get lots of disorganised feelings written down. I wouldn't have written that outpouring if I'd thought for a moment that anyone would read it.

I felt this overflowing sense of guilt. My son hadn't been born yet and I already felt there were so many things for which to judge me. Certain questions arose. How could I translate this into images intuitively, rather than intellectually, to present a cinematic depiction of my inner feelings? How could I keep the moral turmoil within the structure of a piece?

## How was the journal entry transformed into the poem?

Usually there'll be lots of drafts, but this came really quickly. It was almost like a process of translation. There was nothing in terms of the language that I wanted to keep from the early jottings. The one thing I wanted to preserve was that sense of disorganisation through feelings being piled on top of each other.

I'd noticed that in Netflix series there is frequently a certain type of female character, often white, who has an arc where they do some pretty heinous things, then the script allows them to redeem themselves. All of the images in 'The Final Episode' are of that type of character. I'm layering all of their actions on top of each other, making myself feel as bad as possible to see if I can reach a denouement.

I use the idea of games when I'm writing and 'The Final Episode' has a game running through it. You've got the repetition of '*who*' throughout and the image of female characters who gradually merge into one person, until she's finally on the doorstep.

Sometimes people read this and think that I'm saying that all of these actions can be equated with one another and of course they can't. You can't compare someone who kills half a village as a CIA operative with someone who doesn't go into their AA meeting. It doesn't follow a strict pattern, but as the poem goes on, the crimes, or acts, become more and more forgivable – or understandable – until at the end I'm begging for forgiveness.

I like to see my poems as free drafts and they are often a complete mess, but usually my final version will have some resemblance to the first version, which isn't the case here. The words are different, but the emotional heart of the poem is the same. I don't think I've done that since, turned a journal entry into a poem, nor do I think it's something I could replicate as a technique.

**Let's explore some of the specifics of the poem such as the use of sentence fragments, the dialogue and that final address.**

I don't make conscious choices about this type of thing when I'm writing. In fact, I generally only have those kinds of objective thoughts when something *isn't* working, and the voice is stalling the momentum. But with this poem, I felt the tug immediately, and the '*who*' at the beginning of lines felt alive and unfinished, and something about that unfinishedness allowed each line to generate the next, so then I didn't question it. This lends itself to a kind of broken anaphora which determines the form. Sometimes a poem wants you to intervene and lead, and sometimes a poem just wants you to get out of its way.

As for the dialogue, I love dialogue in poems, as it always feels slightly uncalled for and inappropriate – like real voices are entering the poem without my permission and disrupting it. I love the clash between deliberate, woven poetic language and what feels like spontaneous, unbidden bursts.

Regarding the direct address in the last line, the '*you*' in my poems is rarely – perhaps never – a reader in the general sense, it's more intimate and private than that. If I were to analyse, I'd say the '*you*' in the last line makes it a sort of love poem, which, to me, it is. A pitch-black love poem.

**What role does the title play?**

Titles can have lots of different purposes. They can give a clue as to how the reader approaches the poem. 'The Final Episode' is a clue in the way that it makes you read it in terms of television, but is also the sense of growth of the character and what happens in their last episode, focusing on the emotion of the poem.

Or the title can deliberately make the first line a surprise, for example, by being different in tone.

Sometimes a title may not mean much upon first reading,

but will be activated by a reading of the poem. For example, there's a new poem in the collection I'm currently writing called 'The Frozen Aisle', which begins in a supermarket but ends in a graveyard where dead bodies are waiting for judgement day, in a frozen aisle between heaven and the soil.

Alternatively, you can unprepare the reader by giving them a seemingly simple title like Selima Hill's 'Cow', where you're not necessarily trying to do anything with the title apart from be as simple as possible, to usher the reader in and then let the poem overwhelm them.

In my own work, sometimes the title will come immediately, sometimes I'll treat it a bit like trying on hats in a shop and I'll come up with ten different titles with drastically different tones and effects. I'll try them on the poem and then read it and see how it changes and that's fun, because I think if you get it into your head that there's a perfect title, that can be quite intimidating. Whereas if you think there are lots of different hats it could wear that would present it differently, you can enjoy experimenting.

## Can you tell me a little about your use of free verse?

People think that free verse is free, but it isn't. When I'm reading a final draft out loud, I might notice that there are too many syllables on a line. I'm not counting them as such, it's more a case of learning the music of a poem as you're writing it and then adhering to it.

## You devise games as a stimulus for writing.

The feelings to write need to be overwhelming, yet a poem is coming not just from an emotional, but also a playful place. It's created in the tension between the playful and the personal.

First, I clasp onto the feeling, then find the right receptacle to pour it into. I need a game to discover the poem. This could be an image, a first line, a language game or something entirely different.

So, I ask myself what rules I can create and then follow them. Each poem has different rules that you have to learn and if you repeat the same process too many times, it stops working, as you stop having realisations and your poems become too formulaic. You then have to unlearn it and create new rules. There's no other medium where you come a cropper as soon as you start feeling like you know what you're doing!

## Let's talk about your redrafting process.

Writing poetry isn't necessarily linear. Sometimes it takes two months to write a poem. There is a back and forthness between lots of different drafts where I ask myself have I brought it more into focus, or dulled it? I might get to draft fifteen and not like it anymore, but return to draft thirteen and find the emotional arteries of the poem there. It's important that whatever I was feeling in that first draft is not just retained, but also when I read it back to myself, I can feel it anew.

The gulf between a finished and a nearly finished poem can widen and sometimes be pretty vast. There may be one line that's dishonest, but never in the same way. It's not like fixing a car, where you can learn how to do it.

## How do you know which drafts to discard and which to pursue?

A first draft has to make me feel uncomfortable, or that I'm taking a risk in some way. I explore how far I can push an idea, or a game, or an image, until the poem starts talking back to me and telling me something I didn't already know. I start lots and lots of poems that don't go any further. It's like throwing out a rope and you keep writing until you can feel a tug on the other end. This poem wants to exist. You don't necessarily want to know where it'll end or what's going to happen, but you need to suddenly feel that tug that the poem wants to exist.

Sometimes I'll think I've got a great opening and I'll write out into it, but sometimes it just goes slack, either emotionally or there isn't something compelling enough about the image. When that happens, you can rewrite it as much as you like, make it look as neat as you like, make it look beautiful, but it's like giving mouth-to-mouth to a log. You can't fake it.

## What are your writing strengths?

Teaching. I love teaching and it gives me the opportunity to articulate my process in different ways, enabling me to see it as supporting my writing to constantly evolve.

## Can you identify any weaknesses within your writing?

I feel that I have an overattachment to a particular type of speaker and keep returning to the same voice. I want to challenge myself by stretching out of certain tropes, for example where I present myself as unenlightened and the bad guy.

I ask myself questions. Have I done this before? Am I being brave or merely impersonating my previous bravery? I don't want my poems to be safe.

## Several of the poems in this book are rooted in trauma. How much influence does suffering have on creativity?

This poem comes from my collection, *'The Air Year'*, which I wrote feverishly over an intense seven-month period. I was staying up till four o'clock in the morning and sometimes writing two poems in a day.

There were a lot of things going on in my personal life at once, pain and confusion, and writing is both a way of processing, but probably also a way of avoiding. I think sometimes it's easier to be a poet than a person. If I was writing about it, I could at least feel that I was creating from the destruction.

It's not fashionable now to say you need pain to create, and it isn't always the truth, but sometimes it can completely light this fire inside you. Lucie Brock-Broido said, 'A poem is troubled into its making. It's not like a thing that blooms; it's a thing that wounds,' and for '*The Air Year',* that's completely how it was built. It's also why the poems speak to each other, not because I was intending to link them thematically, but because I was writing them from the same storm.

'The Final Episode' was actually one of the last poems I wrote for the collection and by that point, I'd tuned in to a certain kind of language and I felt quite powerful that I could jump in and write a final draft, but I can't do that now which is great for me personally, but I'm not firing on all cylinders.

## What advice would you offer to emerging poets?

Never be afraid of writing rubbish. When you're writing a metaphor, don't think of it as a metaphor, believe your own images. Immerse yourselves in the words of a poem, no matter how silly they might seem. You never really know where a poem is taking you. A poem about a paperclip may lead you to the death of your mother. Let the poem show the way.

## Do you have any favourite poets from your childhood?

When I was thirteen, someone gave me the '*Selected Poems of James Tate*' and it blew my mind. The words felt so alive with humour, violence, sadness and playfulness. I immediately thought that this was the language that I could speak, and I carried it around with me, like a Bible, for several years.

# GEORGE SZIRTES
# HOW TO PLAY YOUR INTERNAL ORGANS OVERNIGHT 12

*How to Play Your Internal Organs Overnight 9*
*(Early Draft)*

The body seems to die but lives again,
so in the music, deep inside the form,
a cell begins to multiply and strain

towards a form inside both mind and brain
so it may seem that cells are uniform
and things that seem to die begin again.

They die once, then once more. The living chain
of memory can keep a body warm
though cells still gather, multiply and strain.

One dies in childbirth, one under a train,
one in a flood, another in a storm.
When bodies die they seem to live again.

How can a body that's alive explain
the reasons why a body comes to harm,
however bodies multiply and strain

to find a shelter from the constant rain,
how birth and rebirth constitute the norm
as things appear to die but live again
and bodies gather, multiply and strain.

## THE PROCESS OF POETRY

*How to Play Your Internal Organs Overnight 12*
*(Final Version)*

The whole thing seems to die but starts again,
so in the music, deep inside the form,
a cell begins to multiply and strain

towards a form inside both mind and brain
so it may seem that themes are uniform
and things that seem to die can live again.

It dies once, then once more. The living chain
of memory can keep dead bodies warm
though cells still gather, multiply and strain.

One dies in childbirth, one under a train,
one in a flood, another in a storm,
yet things that seem to die can live again.

Familiar body! How can you explain
the reasons that a body comes to harm,
however bodies multiply and strain

to find a shelter from the constant rain,
how birth and rebirth constitute the norm
as things appear to die but start again
and bodies gather, multiply, and strain.

## What was the impetus for this poem?

It was written as part of a collaborative project initiated by Steven Fowler, who introduced unknown poets to one another with the aim of producing a series of poems, sparked by responses to pieces of music. I was paired with Andrew McDonnell, who provided me with musical prompts for each poem and I did likewise for him. For this particular poem, the stimulus was a composition with the rather unusual title, 'How to Play Your Internal Organs Overnight'.

## How many drafts did you write and how did the subject of the poem emerge?

The poem was written over twelve drafts and its progression is shown in the titles.

It began with music. However, listening to the music over and over led to thoughts about how the body, like music, is composed of small units that reproduce themselves. Music is also like the body in terms of repetition and heartbeat.

The whole poem is, in effect, seeking a balance between music and the body. The difficulty is ensuring that it doesn't become exclusively about the body or exclusively about music. Neither did I want it to become too abstract through the use of technical musical terms.

There are several notions of death in it. When I initially introduced the image of the body, it felt rather abstract, then, in a later version, it became the body of my mother, but that seemed too much of a shock so I took it out. That was not where the emotional roots of the poem began. Later, in the fourth stanza, there is a suggestion of various deaths from different causes. Nevertheless, the shadow of my mother remained.

**Often the word changes may be related to sound, rhythm, or specificity, but here the most significant influence is the subject matter.**

Yes, it was a matter of emphasis. It started with the piece of music in which the theme was constantly revised, and, at that point, I began to think of the body, but it didn't feel quite right to be starting with that, so I thought I would start with the idea of the music, then lead into the body.

In terms of word choice, '*the body*' became the broader '*whole thing*' so as to keep open the possibility of music as the prime subject. Similarly, '*lives again*' became '*starts again*' and '*cells*', again clearly very body orientated, became the more musically orientated '*themes*'. At the beginning of the third stanza, '*It*' replaces '*they*' since the focus is still on music, although it is on the point of morphing into the idea of the body.

The dialogue is, therefore, between music and body, but memory is also a factor. That's where the idea of my own mother's body emerged. The lines, '*The living chain/ of memory can keep dead bodies warm*' suggests that we have the power of keeping various people, not just one specific person, '*alive*' in our thoughts and memories. So '*the body*' could refer to them.

**A striking change occurs in the fifth stanza with the direct address, '*Familiar body!*'**

That refers not merely to my mother's body, but also to my own, or, for that matter, the body of anyone familiar with us. It is a reminder to me – to us all – that we are mortal. This phrase retains a degree of human warmth for my mother.

Adding '*you*' later in this line, is a way of addressing the reader, but, as I hear it, it applies to me too. In other words, it serves a double function. I could have used '*one*' rather than '*you*' but that would have been too distancing. Conversely, '*we*' assumes too much of a community with the reader, while '*you*' invites intimacy but does not identify us too closely with each other.

## Clearly editing doesn't just apply to the words or structure, but also to the punctuation.

I rarely use exclamation marks, but here, one draws attention to a phrase I only included in the very final draft when it became clear that it was essential to the poem. *'Familiar body!'* is a realisation of my own mortality. The exclamation mark says: wake up, this isn't an abstract discussion, this is about you. Its appearance was a surprise, and I like surprises.

I made one further change to the punctuation in the final line, introducing a comma between *'multiply'* and *'strain'*. I wanted to split the two words into two distinct actions. That way it would feel less glib.

## What are the constraints and benefits of a strict form such as a villanelle?

The villanelle is one of the most artificial and ceremonial of forms, but I wanted neither artifice nor ceremony. As the final drafts stands, it skates close to both, but I was hoping to avoid that.

Regarding the whole idea of constraint, some people think it locks you up, but I think it can offer unexpected freedoms and possibilities: you may discover something much better than you originally intended. You may know the number of lines required, the rhyme scheme and so forth, but you don't know what possibilities arise when you are forced to invent in order to meet requirements. Working with requirements is a form of dance: a dance, a negotiation, with language.

The villanelle is, in fact, rather more adaptable than we think. Dylan Thomas raging against the dying of the light, William Empson's sense of rottenness at the core of things, and Elizabeth Bishop's mourning for the tragic loss of her friend and lover are all villanelles. Something in the very form with its repetitions, suggests obsession. Whatever that is, it has to be gnawing at the poem. It is that which holds it together. For me, in this case, it is my mother's death, and the realised sense of the fragility of the human body.

## Is your creative process based on intellect or instinct?

Writing, for me, is like entering a fast machine. Having made a choice of subject and first line, no fully rational thought is involved after that. The whole thing is more intuitive. The poem moves and lurches in the dance, until there's no distinction between craft and instinct. Craft becomes instinct. Instinct drives everything ultimately, even in something as formal as a villanelle.

Surprisingly perhaps, I have never been systematic. What I love about writing is the entry into a mood where one bumps up against words and phrases. The first two lines are important, but I don't know where they will lead me. Nor am I particularly concerned. I am in the dance. That is what matters.

## Did you have a favourite poet as a child?

I went to art school rather than university and had read hardly any poetry in English as an immigrant child. Later, in my senior school library, when I was sixteen or seventeen, I'd pick poetry books off the shelves, and dwell on all that white space around the words, words that seemed to prod fascinating worlds into motion. It may not be irrelevant that I was supposed to be revising Physics at the time. Poetry was the ultimate distraction.

## Poetry may often feel like a solitary pursuit, but you have been involved in several collaborations.

I have collaborated with different people over a number of years and each collaboration has been an enriching experience, enabling me to broaden my work.

In 2015, I collaborated with Carol Watts. We didn't know each other at all and were only supposed to be writing eight minutes' worth of performance but we ended up writing a 56-page book. We started by ringing each other. At the end of our first conversation, I asked Carol what her favourite length of poem was. When she said that it was 28 lines, I queried whether this was because that was the length of two sonnets. No, she explained. The length was determined by the number of lines you could fit onto a piece of paper.

Very few of my collaborations start off with a particular topic. Carol soon found a subject, but she didn't tell me what it was, so I simply read her first 28-line poem and picked up elements in it that might serve for my own 27-line poem. Having written it, I sent that to her, in response to which she then wrote a 26-line poem and so we went on. We got down to one line, then found we were enjoying it so much we worked our way back to 28 again, so that made 56 in all. The book was titled '*Fifty-Six*', partly because that was the total number of poems and partly because of the complete coincidence that I came to England as a refugee in 1956. Carol being a very different kind of poet, I learned a lot from her. I remain deeply grateful for the experience.

Another partnership involved an exchange of poems with the outstanding Singaporean poet, Alvin Pang. This took the form of a year-long correspondence about our individual experiences of Covid. We went through a whole gamut of forms in the course of that. I loved it. The book, titled '*Diaphanous*', should come out soon.

I also began a collaboration with poet and academic, Tiffany Atkinson, writing crime fiction in formal sonnets. We wrote around 45 sonnets but haven't finished it yet.

Now there is yet another collaboration with Hungarian poet and scholar, Katalin Szlukovényi, in the form of ten-line postcards from Europe. We translate each other's poems as we go.

## Can poetry be a means of challenging the world and its politics?

There's a long tradition of poetry that challenges authority, institutions, and power generally, often through satire. Revolutionary verse requires the right historical circumstances and good satire is far from easy to write. You need to know how to deploy irony, wit and hyperbole. It can take a good deal of courage too.

**You first language is Hungarian. Does writing in a second language offer unexpected benefits?**

There are interesting theories about second language writing but it's difficult to apply theories to oneself. It is possible that writing in a second language renders the writer more sensitive to the levels and ambiguities of that language. One has to learn and to listen more closely to register, tone, and implication. Everything is new and strange. There may be something useful in that for writing poetry.

**As well as being a prolific poet, you also translate the work of other poets. Can we explore how something as nuanced as poetry works in a different language?**

Translating is a way of understanding and conveying complexities in lives removed from your own. I personally try to hear what's going on in the original poem or prose and hope to make my translation sound as close as possible to what I hear in the original. Ideally, I'd like to produce a poem in my language that the original writer would recognise as theirs.

**What advice do you offer your students?**

I tend to offer suggestions, not rules. Here are a few things at random.

I ask students to consider the voice of the poem, its relation to their own speaking voice, to think about its register, and to ensure that it remains consistent throughout the poem.

I suggest they ask themselves whether the line they are writing moves the poem along rather than stalls it or diverts it. That might become clearer after several drafts.

In terms of narrative structure, I suggest to them that a good many poems – not all by any means – consist of three stages of development. It is worthwhile listening out for that possibility in the poems they read and also in those they write.

Three stages seem to provide a stable structure. I usually start by considering the structure of the classical ode (strophe, antistrophe, epode) and look to demonstrate how far that is echoed in other, perfectly modern poems.

Endings are important too; *End firmly and step off lightly* is an idea I would put before them. Brief mottoes like that are memorable. As a young poet, I was fortunate enough to be informally mentored by Peter Porter, whose advice on drafts was: *When you've got the building, remove the scaffolding.* I have never forgotten that.

Most of all it is vital to listen to what you are saying, to say it aloud, and to feel the shape of language in your hands.

## What skills does a poet require?

You don't need to be brilliant or scholarly, or even hair-trigger sensitive, but you must believe in the delight of the act. That is not always easy, because there are times when nothing comes and you are struggling. A keen ear, an ability to flow with a detected tide, a musician's skill, a dancer's skill, these are your tools. You must also have resilience. If, after several attempts, a poem seems to be dead, screw it up and put it in the bin. After all, it's just a piece of paper. But, having done that, go on.

# LIZ LOCHHEAD
# CHIMNEYSWEEPERS

*The Naming of The Flowers, Late May*
*(Early Draft)*

> *Golden lads and girls all must*
> *As chimney-sweepers come to dust.*
> William Shakespeare: Cymbeline

A fool's errand to be carrying home
this bunch of the dandelion clocks
Shakespeare called *chimney-sweepers*
and Gordon's email from Mull says
his wee grand-daughter calls *puff-balls* --
but I'm holding my breath, and them, this carefully
because I want to take them home and try
to paint them although
one puff of wind and – in no time –
I'll be stuck with nothing but a hank of
leggy, limp, milky *pee-the-bed*
stalks topped with baldy wee green buttons.

On daisy hill by the railway bridge
sits a girl weaving a blue-bell chain

that hangs heavy as a rope till she loops it,
a coronet upon her hair,
hair so glossy I note it's *nut brown*.
I'm wondering is this to be her *something blue?*

We call out to each other
as folk do in these times of separation and distancing
and she asks me what I'm doing with the dead dandelions?

I can hardly believe it when she says
she never in all her childhood
told the time by a dandelion clock.

She's up to her oxters in ox-eye daisies,
the ones my mother, Margaret,
always called *Marguerites* but never
without telling me again how my father,
writing to her from France before Dunkirk or after D. Day
always began his letters
*Dear Marguerite.*

Oh Mum,
Mum who never got to be as old as I am now,
Oh Mum, how much I wish today I could ask you,
"Mum, did you ever hear tell of this strange superstition
this girl just told me? How a maiden crowned
by a chain woven out of bluebells can never tell a lie?"

THE PROCESS OF POETRY

## *Chimneysweepers (Final Version)*

Maytime and I'm
on a fool's errand
carrying home this bunch of the dandelion clocks
which Shakespeare called *chimneysweepers*
and a friend tells me his wee grand-daughter
in the here-and-now calls *puffballs*.
I'm holding my breath, and them, this carefully
because I want to take them home and try
to paint them, although
one breath of wind and in no time
I'll be stuck with nothing but a hank of
leggy, limp, milky pee-the-bed stalks
topped with baldy wee green buttons, for
*golden lads and girls all must*
*as chimneysweepers come to dust.*


On daisy hill by the railway bridge
one lone pair of lovers laze in the sun.
A little apart from her, he lounges
smoking a slow cigarette and waits
smiling, half-watching her weave a bluebell chain
that swings intricate from her fingers, hangs heavy
till she loops it, a coronet upon her nut-brown hair.
I'm wondering is this to be her *something blue?*

She calls out to me, I to her,
as folk do in these days of distancing

and I can hardly believe it when she says
she never in all her childhood
told the time by a dandelion clock.

She's up to her oxters in ox-eye daisies, this girl.
The ones my mother, Margaret,
always called *marguerites* but never
without telling me again how my father
writing to her from France before Dunkirk or after D. Day
always began his letters *Dear Marguerite.*

*The saying goes that a maiden*
*crowned by bluebells can never tell a lie*
the girl informs me, solemn as she
crosses her fingers, each hand held high,
the smoke from her lover's cigarette
almost but not quite as blue as
the frail blooms -- time, truth and a promise -- that she
braided together on this their one-and-only
sure to be perfect Summer's day.

Oh *Marguerite   Margaret   my Mum*
who never got to be as old as I am today
did you ever hear tell of this proverb?
Oh Mum how much I wish I could ask you
this and so many other
small and silly things, but
*golden lads and girls all must*
*as chimneysweepers come to dust.*

## How did the poem originate?

I began writing it in 2020 during the first lockdown of the Covid pandemic. Like so many others then, I was concerned about time and its passing.

This poem is based on a real incident. In it, I'm trying to capture the essence of one particular day in May 2020, when the weather was scorching hot and, on my permitted exercise hour, I was walking past a piece of urban waste ground near my home in Glasgow. For me, it's '*daisy hill*' as – for a week or so at the end of May – it's carpeted all over with those big ox-eye daisies, *marguerites*. Stunning. Back then, I was obsessed with trying to carry wee bunches of dandelion clocks, handfuls of fragile flyaway time, safely home to put them in vessels of some sort for still life arrangements and to paint them.

That day as I passed, a young woman, a stranger, bonny, sitting almost submerged in that sea of great big daisies, was making something I'd never seen before, a chain of *bluebells*. Normally you don't talk to people passing you in a city street, but it was different in lockdown. She called out to me, wanting to know what I was doing with the dead dandelions. I was amazed to discover that she had never heard of dandelion clocks, had never told the time with one in her childhood.

The girl in the poem has her whole life in front of her, whereas the poem's first-person narrator is old. She must be, as, in this case, the person telling the story is *me*, whereas my narrators are often very different from me – it's long been normal for me to write in different voices and personae. The 'I' in a poem of mine is quite unlikely to be autobiographical.

During lockdown, I was reading a biography of Keats, his letters and his poems, including 'La Belle Dame Sans Merci' and 'The Eve of Saint Agnes', which I first fell in love with when I was fourteen and was yet, in real life, to fall in love. But longing to! Keats writes this in the third person. It's a romance, mock mediaeval, the story of chaste fair Madeline; of her longing for her lover-to-be Porphyro; and the good and brave, if ancient and palsied, Angela, '*the sole/old beldame weak in body and in soul*', the facilitator who helps the lovers to elope.

These are my '*beldame*' years. I am conscious that I am now four years older than my mother was when she died at the age of seventy-one. This poem of mine is, I now realise, in part me accepting that I'm old, a '*beldame*', a bystander, someone at best on the side of lovers, but a lover no more.

One is always aware of Keats dying at twenty-five and Burns at thirty-seven. Poetry and longevity often don't go together. Although when I'm writing a poem, rarely am I aware of writing a sequence – no, I am just focusing on that particular piece – looking back, I realise I did in fact write, over as many months, drafts of three or four *other* poems about time passing and mortality. Natural processes. If these poems do form an accidental sequence, it's not at all a gloomy one I hope!

## Over what period of time was 'Chimneysweepers' written?

I began it in Summer 2020. I don't call it redrafting; I just tinker and tweak till it's done. There is no typical timescale, and I can't tell you exactly how many changes I made to this poem, but I do know that it was far more than usual and spread over more than two and a half years to boot. Verses that suddenly really weren't working for me were rewritten over Summer 2021. It got a good going over once again in November 2022. In very early March 2023, I came back to it and I know now it is as close as I'll ever get to what I wanted it to be and I won't touch it again.

## Even the title and epigraph evolved as the poem progressed?

Thinking of the poem 'The Naming of Parts', I initially thought that 'The Naming of the Flowers, Late May' was the right title. However, when I shared a half-written draft (which might even have been then a failed experiment in prose) with a friend of mine, the short story writer, Helen Simpson, she reminded me that Shakespeare had called dandelion clocks 'chimneysweepers' and I realised right there that this was

the right title. I was fascinated that Shakespeare could take
a dialect word, a Warwickshire word, and, because of the
force of his poetic imagination it would then be enshrined in
meaning throughout the entire English language. Shakespeare
uses it as a single word, un-hyphenated, so I have done the
same.

(I only hope 'up to her *oxters* in ox-eye daisies' works like that
too, but I knew right from the start that, dialect word or not,
Scots word or not, I was using it.)

Shakespeare's 'golden lads and girls' couplet from 'Cymbeline'
was initially an epigraph for my poem. I love the spare
folksong quality of Shakespeare's songs, almost more than
I love his sonnets even. However, as my poem developed,
his words assumed a greater significance and were moved
from its original position as a mere epigraph to become a
repeated chorus, an integral part of my poem itself. Seduced
by both the vivid image and the philosophical melancholy of
Shakespeare's familiar couplet, I chose to steal it and quote it
quite shamelessly in the body of my poem.

## Let's explore the development of the poem.

I made several changes, occasionally adding a word or an
image, but also omitting lines. Occasionally these might be
re-instated later. Sometimes you can't explain to yourself why
you've made a change, all you can say is you did so because you
like it better. Simple as.

The biggest change between the two versions you have read
here – it happened very early on, I think in the very next
draft – was to add in the girl's lover. He is just off to the side
and smoking, says nothing, but he has to be there. If you don't
create a character *in words,* they are simply not present in the
poem. The girl has to be not just a young girl but a potential
bride, if the bluebell chain is to be that *'something blue'*.

You are making a world when you're making a poem, it's
*physical.* You've got to get the voice of the poem down in black
and white so that it lives and speaks to everybody. You hope.

The images are what's important and you need to find exactly the right and most simple words to embody them.

'*Maytime*' was part of the original title and, when the title changed, I included it in the first line of the poem itself, to nail that sense of merry-month-of-May Spring and give an appropriate folk-loric feel to it.

I could see the girl smiling, but no wonder I hated the way I'd at one time described this and in quite a late version too! '*She smiles all her Summer at her lover*'. Embarrassingly bad. That just had to go.

## Can we explore the final stanza?

As I was about to give it to a publication in March 2023, I found a version from July 2021 whose last stanza contained two or three things I had since lost, but which I now felt strongly that the poem needed. One of these was my mother's three identities, Margaret, Marguerite and my Mum, which reflect the shifting times of her life. She was *Margaret* to her parents, her family and others; *Marguerite* to my father (in letters from him in the army in France during the war); and, of course, *my Mum* to me.

Questioning my Mum in the poem dramatised the impossibility of asking her anything at all anymore. It's the pain of the tiny little things that you'd love to ask someone, but can't, isn't it?

## How did you know when it was finished?

The Russian writer, Isaac Babel, said something like, 'You know you've finished when having gone through it taking out all of the commas, you find yourself going back and reinstating them.' I found this felt true when, on re-reading earlier drafts, I reinstated small fragments of text that seemed to me to reintroduce certain lost key ideas into the final version. Suddenly, the words those '*frail blooms – time, truth and a promise*' felt as if *they wrote themselves*. It had been a long time coming, this feeling which poets depend on. The word '*blooms*' contains the sound of *blue*. They now were both blossoms and also as blue as bluebells are. With '*braided together*' I knew that the language was finally gelling. I thought: It feels clear. At last. Stop. That's how I know it's definitely finished now.

## What role does the truth play in a poem and how important is it to be factually accurate?

The only thing I made up here is the girl crossing her fingers, everything else is exactly what I saw and experienced that day. Not that this matters at all.

That lover was essential not just because he was present that day – which he was – but to give a reason for the '*something blue*'. A potential bridegroom? He's not the key focus of the story though. The drama is between the narrator and the young woman, and between the absence of the narrator's dead mother and herself.

Sometimes the literal truth isn't relevant. '*Gordon*', who is named in the first draft (as is '*Mull*', where he happens to live) – both these details are the factual truth, but unnecessary. He appears in the final version, properly, as simply 'a friend'. What's not essential mars the poem. Always.

## You have been commissioned to write poems to a specific brief in various capacities, including as Makar. How different is this process?

It's totally different. During my time as Makar, I was sometimes asked to come up with a poem for an occasion. I always managed this, given a clear brief and a reasonable deadline.

However, sometimes a poem being demanded of me gave me the impetus to write a piece on a theme I would never have thought of and to surprise myself. In fact, some of my commissioned pieces have become favourite poems of mine. I had to write a poem for Commonwealth Day, for example, which I had to read at Westminster Abbey. This was a very enjoyable experience, but more importantly I still think it is a good poem. A tough poem. Worth publishing.

Other times though, I was less happy with the result. I was asked to write a poem to perform as part of the Opening of the Scottish Parliament. I did my best. It worked fine for the event, but I cut it down significantly to song-length when I published it. I wish I'd had the time to do this before its original out-loud outing.

In one instance – long before the Makar days - I had to write for a BBC Education Programme 'a dialect poem' to encourage children to 'at least in their *creative* writing' keep using '*hometown English*'. It was about 35 years ago, but I still remember how stuck I was. It was murder. The day before it was due, I made gallons of tea and stayed up all night. The result is one of my most popular poems which I still perform.

### Is it easier to write in free verse?

Definitely not. Given that initial wee bit of an idea for what the poem is trying to say has arrived (and *if* it seems to want to come to being in a regular form, rhyme or metre), it's a lot easier to write this than it is to write in free verse. The form and the metre and the rhyme itself provide not just structure but meaning itself. In a free verse poem there are, initially, no rules. The 'rules' certainly do emerge as one writes but are only useful for this one poem.

### How do you approach your writing?

I love writing when I'm writing, and I hate it when I can't do it. Which is often. I write by hand and type up when I've got a first draft. Often they don't go any further than that and many of them end up in the bin. You do have to murder your darlings, but the problem is you don't know initially which are these darlings who need to be for the chop...

### Did you have a favourite poet as a child?

I focus more on individual poems more than I do on poets. Anon is the best ever. I loved Burns's 'To a Mouse' which I learnt off by heart as a wee girl. Still do. Another favourite poem when I was nine or ten was 'Meg Merrilies'. It's by Keats, who I still love (and whose influence is so strong in 'Chimneysweepers')

## What advice would you give to emerging poets?

Read poems you love. Read poems you love but don't necessarily understand. Keep writing. Keep writing what you don't necessarily understand. Strive to gradually understand it and to make it (somehow) clear. While leaving room for mystery. Just do it and keep doing it. If a poem begins to come, always make the time to put it down on paper, however roughly. Don't try and keep it in your head. It'll evaporate.

# THE LION
# MONA ARSHI

*The Lion (Early Draft)*

**The Lion**

How unstable and exotic he is now.
Lion is so old he has snacks sent up
via means of a pulley.

Although you never really quite
master the deep language of a lion,
I am made dumb by the rough stroke
of his tongue upon mine.

Nowadays I make allowances. When we
lie together I hear the crackle of his bones
and when I bring myself to open my eyes
he's weeping, in the candle-light his pupils

resemble dark embroidered felt circles.
Sometimes I think that all I am is a comfort
blanket for his arthritic mouth. But then
there are those evenings when he can

name every flower in the garden and
make fingers of light dance for me behind the
drapery. He's always saying he wants to draw me.

He starts undressing me under the sweetening stars.
Understand this he says, this might be the last time that
I will see how the thin light enters you.

## *The Lion (Final Version)*

How unstable and old he is now.
Lion, like God, has snacks sent up

by means of a pulley. Although
you can never master the deep language

of Lion. I am made dumb by the rough
stroke of his tongue upon mine.

Nowadays I make allowances. We lie
together and I hear the crackle of his bones

and when I bring myself to open my eyes
he weeps, his pupils resembling dark

embroidered felt circles. Sometimes
I think all I am is a comfort blanket for his

arthritic mouth. But many evenings he'll sit
twisted behind the drapery solving my

vulgar fractions with nothing but his claws.
Lion and I break bread; I tend to his mane and

he sets a thousand scented fuses under my skin.
He starts undressing me under the sweetening stars.

*Please girl*, he mews; this might be the last time
I will see how the thin light enters you.

## You came to poetry by a rather unusual route.

Yes, I was a human rights lawyer and writing poetry is the polar opposite of writing a rule-bound legal discourse. However, the two share the same restless interrogation of language. Furthermore, I am a very good editor of my own work where I bring in my lawyer skillset.

When I was pregnant with my daughters, I was advised to rest. I started reading a lot of poetry and instantly felt at home. I feel that poetry is a counterweight to the busy, fast, inattentive world in which we live. The rewards of poetry are astronomical. You're transmuting the world into language and a poetic line is unique, in that it can hold the most unimaginable pain or exquisite pleasure.

## Can you tell me about the origins of the poem?

This is one of my early poems and was in my first collection, '*Small Hands*'. Its concerns are the linguistic and sexual tussles in a relationship, the texture and material of language, and who has agency in a relationship.

## How long did it take to complete and do you have an idea which early draft this is?

I wrote this poem over a year. I do so many drafts it's difficult to remember exactly which one this is, but it's probably around the seventh or eighth. I then went on to write another ten or so versions and after that my editor, Deryn Rees-Jones, also made some changes.

## One striking difference is to the form.

Form isn't a mechanical exercise, it's also a large part of the process. This poem has gone from an unprincipled form and at this point, I'm trying to find my way in. Even the music is out, probably as I didn't read it out sufficiently. Reading it aloud is fundamental. Hearing a poem in the air of the world is a fundamental part of the process. In that early draft it feels clunky and 'prosey'. The sound gives me a real signal as to what the lineation will be and where the form will be found.

I love couplets. I'm drawn to them because of the tradition of writing love poems in couplets, and this is a love poem, albeit a subversive one. However, I didn't want closed couplets. There's some slightly unusual lineation which subverts the reader's expectations. For example, '*Although*' and '*Sometimes*' are both at the end of a line as I want the reader to slow down and open up to the next line.

## Let's explore some of the other developments within the poem, for example, the addition of '*God*' and the extended religious metaphor.

I was taught that you should resist using abstracts and words like God in a poem, and yet I do it all the time. I spent quite a while thinking about this and, whilst it's perhaps an extreme way of defining a relationship, I feel that some relationships can contain a spiritual dimension and wanted to acknowledge that sense of reverence. I then extended this image to the breaking of bread towards the end of the poem.

The poet and mentor, Mimi Khalvati, advised that if you're not sure what you want to say, put it in prose to start with, and I think that's what I was doing with the '*naming every flower*' line.

The odd thing is that when you're in the midst of writing a poem, you become somehow slightly more open and porous to the world around you. At the time, my young daughters were struggling with vulgar fractions and I thought what a strange and wonderful phrase, maybe my lion might be interested in that and it floated into the poem like that. That's why I always advise everyone to keep their old writing notebooks; you never know what gems you might find!

## Tell us about your editing process.

The initial draft is a kind of intuitive conjuring act. Poetry needs that, it's almost like a holy trinity comprising of you, the writing hand and this third hand. You are channelling and plundering a part of your subconscious.

The initial stage is the magical part: something stirs, some kindling is set alight, something is working in the corner of your eye. Then there's the gathering up of the initial lines, and I like to think of this work as the 'holy trinity', where you have the poet's subconscious, the poet's hand and this sort of other third hand that's sort of mixed it up altogether. This part of writing is where you have to let go and trust the poem a bit. The poem is always wiser than you and you have to step out of it, or make yourself ready to be at service.

Editing is often the most difficult part. I think that listening is a big part of the editing process. The Ear is the best diagnostic tool we have. Only after that can you go in with your little scalpel and trim words to perhaps more effectively set off and detonate an image, or work on syntax and reorder things. Things like lineation have to be attended to. What effect does natural lineation with sense breaks have? Do you need to speed up a poem? These decisions are really about listening to what the poem wants to be.

That's why it's always good to take a long time to write. The poet, Collette Bryce, said it's important to leave a poem for six months in order to become untethered from it and this is sound advice.

## Let's explore the way in which you have edited this particular poem.

I removed the qualifier '*really quite*', and the indefinite article '*a*', as it works better sonically with '*language of lion*', as well as emphasising that there is only the one, specific lion within the poem. I also removed '*more flowers in the garden*' as it was really just prose.

I added the rather sensual line, '*he sets a thousand fuses under my skin*'.

However, the most significant change in the poem comes in the final stanza. It was a conscious decision to move to direct address. It became important to hear the beloved about whom I'm musing. '*Said*' becomes '*mews*' which is a beautiful word and close to '*muse*'. It echoes with might and light, lends musicality and makes it much more lyrical. As well as giving him a voice, these lines now show that there's a vulnerability to Lion too, which is an essential element of the poem.

## Do you jot down notes when you're out and about?

Yes, definitely. I always have my phone and a notebook with me. I find that when I write on the phone, I use very short lines which become embedded and it then becomes difficult to extend them. Therefore I use my notebook, which is an A4 size, more now, so that I can write longer lines and this overcomes the problem.

## Can you describe life as a working poet and mother?

I write a lot of poems but actually only about half are published. I mostly learn from the poems that aren't necessarily good enough to be published and the annoying poems are the ones that fail and you really can't understand why. I try not to think about publication (though it's hard not to!) but just try and commit to the poem and its journey.

I try not to think about writer's block, but to avoid it, I try and have several poems at different stages of the life cycle, one maybe incubating, another at the editing stage and yet another gathered but formless, I think that makes you feel connected to the work.

I try to connect with poetry every day by either reading poetry itself, reading about it or writing it. However, motherhood is a gift which has a huge impact on my life and priorities. If I have a sick daughter who is running a temperature, she is my central concern, not the poem.

## What are the main themes within your poems?

It's very difficult to talk about your themes in your own work and I let readers decide what the poems are occupied with. Of course, there are certain concerns that I write about, poetry is a magnet for feeling, love in all its aspects and reverie and the role of language are the concerns of most poets I know.

### How does writing in your second language impact on your work?

My first language is Punjabi, it's my 'mother tongue' if you like. I don't think this fact impacts my work directly but I have always been careful with words and language and hypervigilant about using words correctly.

### As a judge for poetry competitions, including The Forward Prize and the TS Eliot Award, it would be interesting to know what you look for in a poem.

The poems that leap out are the poems where there's an element of surprise, not within the subject matter itself necessarily, but within the language. I'm looking for something that keeps me awake at night and that I have to read again. I'm a sucker for metaphor and image. I also appreciate carefulness within a poem in relation to language and lineation.

### Can we explore the intersection between poetry and prose?

Prose feels like a different room in the house to poetry. Having written two collections of poetry and one novel, I would say they come from wildly different places. Poems come from the peripheral space, they infer and nudge their way into being, whereas prose is more direct and you need to attend to it in a different way.

### What advice would you give to developing poets?

Read extensively. Read the canon, read contemporary poetry, read poetry in translation. Read poets writing about their craft and try to understand why a particular poem you like works. Poetry is a unique and incredible art form, it relies on its readers and not just its writers. If you want to be a poet there's a commitment to the long game and rarely any short cuts, I'm afraid.

# JACOB SAM-LA ROSE
# CREDIT DUE

## *Coin Op (Early Draft)*

Used to be, all the best chippies had one. Less than a pound for a wrapped clutch, small portion, a change left over for a life or three. 50p for a credit, a pound for three. In the old days, Bison had to be defeared before anyone else became available. What did that teach you? Conquest. Tenacity. Th nobody's pockets are infinitely deep. That there's always more game than your capacity to play. An that even if you can beat the game, there's always someone that can beat it better than you.

## *Coin Op (Final Version)*

Those days, my list of cornerstone truths
began with drum n' bass, and the fact that
   there would always be
a chip shop open in a lonely street— its light
and signage testament against closing hour
   and any fallen dark—
and in that chip shop: coin-op cabinet,
a waypoint for the lost, aimless and hungry,
   squat in corner, Buddha
of appetite and emptiness. Bless the lottery of dumb
and broken controller stick, perhaps a careworn button
   mashed to senselessness. Bless
the different ways to slice a single coin,
a loser subbed in for every second round. Bless
   leader-board and high scoresheet,
whoever cared enough to mark the time
with their initials, bless the hallowed AAA,
   and all the screens
we poured ourselves into. Bless
those nights,
   our small-change lives.

# THE PROCESS OF POETRY

## What inspired this poem?

Between 2009-2011 I was exploring popular culture in my writing, and aspects that particularly connected with my lived experience. These included different styles of music and the culture of gaming that provided a backdrop to my mid and late teens.

Coincidentally, I came across an article in *The New Yorker* on console gaming and the violence, mortality and the potential for grappling with grief in video games such as 'Halo' and 'Call of Duty'. My own experience of gaming both resonated with and extended beyond what was detailed in that article, sparking a line of thinking that ultimately resulted in the early drafts of this poem.

I grew up in the early to mid-Nineties. Some of the most compelling gaming experiences weren't just about sitting in front of a screen in your own front room; gaming was communal. You had to be somewhere with huge arcade machines, noise, lights and people. I snuck out to the Trocadero Centre and Namco Wonder Park behind Piccadilly Circus. I wanted to capture this sense of a place of gathering, not just for the gaming but for a shared experience.

## How long was the poem written over and which drafts are we exploring?

This is a poem that lived with me for quite a while. I started it in 2009 and it arrived at a final form around 2019, when I became aware that I hadn't edited it for a while, but was happy with what it was. Ten years might sound like a long time, but we're talking about poetry.

It underwent around twelve to fifteen drafts, some of which involved quite significant changes and some of which were relatively minor. Over the first three years, the different drafts really pushed it forward, whilst the drafts after that point were more about locking it in.

## Can we talk about the development of the title?

The original title '*Coin-Op*', added to '*cabinet*', had a rhythm and musicality and was the appropriate term for the hardware. However, it didn't capture the trajectory along which the poem was moving, which related to life more broadly and more philosophically beyond the '*cabinet*'. I wanted to depict these arcade games as a sense of escape, not so much from trauma, but from the mundanity of everyday life.

It later became 'Credit Due'. Credit was there from the very first draft where I was exploring the notion of credit being due to something or someone, in other words, acknowledging achievement. I was interested in the language and terminology related to arcade games which worked on this level too, referencing the 'credits' or lives that you pay for when playing these types of games.

## Let's explore the epigraph.

I took the quote directly from Uncyclopedia, which is a satirical Wikipedia and, initially, it was several lines long. It introduces an awareness of the blank canvas upon which you aspire to leave a mark. Completing the game and climbing to the top of the sheet meant a lot in the moment, even if no one else would ever recognise you by the three characters you chose for your moniker.

The epigraph also introduces a sense of humour by elevating the player to an almost God-like status, by using words from the Catholic creed 'Is, was and always will be'.

## Can you give us a broad overview of the poem's development?

The first draft was more focused on the physical environment. In the second draft, it broadened beyond a single chip shop and referenced specific characters, before homing in again and finally becoming a conversation around gaming and its value as a shared experience.

**The question in the first draft was replaced by a series of prayers or invocations 'bless the...' as the poem developed.**

Whilst the overt question has disappeared, the poem now raises some underlying questions. What are the touchstones of our beliefs? What are our rituals? How do those rituals and beliefs help us to cope with our everyday lives?

When I was developing the poem, I was engaging a sense of secular faith and was fascinated by ritual and tradition. This exploration moves into the language and the repeated invocations lend an almost prayer-like quality to the poem. It draws on Catholicism, but also Buddhism and a broad sense of blessing.

**Does the message change as the poem develops?**

Although the drafts are not saying exactly the same thing, there's a continuity and the scene dressing remains very similar. There is something at the core that tries to connect this notion of the personal and the profound.

The first draft was rooted in the concrete experience of being in a Charlton chip shop, including the money that you pay to get '*a life*' to play with (a pound would equal three lives), and the cabinet itself. Here I'm spelling things out more. I'm asking myself that question, 'What did that teach you?' The lesson I landed on was that nobody's pockets are infinitely deep, that there was only a certain amount of money I could afford to feed into the machine. The points were being made quite concretely.

The language of blessing and ritual wasn't present initially. In the final draft, I deepened that thinking and arrived at the sense of this experience within the broader context of life. This certainly evolved as the drafts progressed.

## I'm interested in the layout, which moves through different forms over various drafts.

I started with the prose paragraph, which was simply a note of what I wanted to explore through the poem. From a single block, I moved on to investigate how line breaks might work. Working through line breaks enables me to determine where the unnecessary, or not necessary enough, words and phrases might be. It also helps me to identify how the poem is moving. Using a text editor, I may have explored other stanza lengths, quickly, perhaps even within a single sitting in some of the earlier drafts. Later, in 2017, I experimented with tercets and a rhyming couplet.

I then ask myself, now I have a sense of what the poem is doing and how the poem is working, how can I refine it to what's essential? What actually needs to be there and what is extraneous? There's definitely still a sense of parcelling up the thinking in this final version, by means of the offset lines.

The last draft is me working with everything on a number of different levels, for example, to gain a sense of what the poem is saying, the movement of ideas through the piece, as well as a visual rhythm – how it moves sonically, but also how its visual presence on the page relates to that sense of movement.

## How much is your poetry influenced by your background and personal experience?

A great deal of my collection, *'Breaking Silence'*, was driven by personal experiences or by issues upon which I wanted to comment that existed within my immediate world.

I have had my thematic obsessions. As a male child raised in a family dominated by strong female figures, I've had an interest in interrogating masculinity, archetypal gender roles and definitions of manhood. I am also fascinated by the nature of faith in a secular sense. In *'Breaking Silence'* I wrote a lot about popular culture. Since then, I've taken even more of an interest in technology and ecology. Each theme has its own life cycle.

That said, I'm not solely concerned with exploring lived experience, and there's a distinct thread of my writing that's invested in more speculative, lyrical and language-based drivers.

## You use a number of different tools in the writing process.

I have a taste for process-based working and focus on three different methods: many of my poems start as hand-drawn sketch-notes and diagrams in an app called Concepts. If a poem demands further research, I'll compile details, findings and any phrases that spark for me in mind maps using Mindnode, which facilitates a branched, less linear, approach. For drafting, I employ a text editor, which can export my material to Word or PDF documents to forward on.

I work on a tablet, which offers both portability and modularity, allowing me to imitate an A4 page by switching between portrait and landscape views. I can write freehand using a stylus, draw, add pictures and manipulate ideas easily around the screen. And I can turn to a more traditional keyboard-driven way of working whenever I need to.

## What's the hardest thing about writing a poem?

Finding the balance between what I want to say and discovering what the poem itself wants to say. Is it doing what I want it to do? Does it feel as if the poem is doing what it needs to do?

## As a director of poetry slams, can you tell us the difference between spoken word and writing for the page?

Although I am happy to perform my work, I don't typically write specially for performance and don't consider myself to be a spoken word poet. I am, however, mindful of the different ways of engaging with poetry. In performance, for example, an audience only gets to hear the poem in that moment. They may have one linear experience of that poem, rather than the luxury of being able to read over a text numerous times, go back to a line and absorb an image at their own pace. They have to ride through that poem with you, so any performance of it serves to curate their experience.

It's probably also important to underline that slams don't necessarily have to favour performance poetry. Slams can simply create communal spaces for poets to share poems and establish some shared considerations as to how to appreciate or value those poems. There's space to celebrate all the various denominations of poetry.

**You do a lot of work in schools. What would your advice to students be on writing their own poetry?**

There is a balance between celebrating, yet also challenging what it is that you do as a writer and poet. Appreciate your individual voice and your unique perspective, whilst recognising the importance of being transformed by feedback and external influences.

Naturally, engage with poetry in whatever form speaks to you as much as you can, not to drown out your own voice, but in order to gain an appreciation of the diverse range of voices that exist in the world of poetry. In time, you can add your own.

There's so much that we can learn by engaging with other people's poetry, while appreciating what our own poetry can be capable of. Try to challenge yourself beyond your instant likes and fascinations in order to expand that sense of what is possible for your own writing.

The key skills you require are care, tenacity and the ability to play. A poet also requires the capacity to live with uncertainty, to strike out on a journey without knowing what the destination will be, but to have faith in the journey regardless.

## As an editor at Flipped Eye Publishing, what do you seek in a submission?

I look for something which excites and challenges me. I'm a reader as well as an editor and I want to be surprised, drawn in and moved in some way. I don't just want to be intellectually stimulated.

I consider myself to be a developmental editor, so I constantly ask myself what it is that I can offer this work and how I myself might need to challenge my biases and beliefs in order to support the best vision of the work. Ultimately, it's very much about discovering new work that represents an opportunity for growth and development.

## Did you have a favourite poet as a child?

When I was thirteen, I enjoyed Seamus Heaney and Alice Walker, who both spoke to me in different ways. I was introduced to the former by my English teacher and my mother had an Alice Walker collection on her bookshelf.

# JOELLE TAYLOR
# ROUND SIX *the body as haunted house*

### *Body As Cemetery: An Extract from C+nto (Early Draft)*

My body is a haunted house/ my mother is in the back room and cannot hear me/ my elder brother takes me to one side and shouts his alarm/ but his voice is blurred/ wading through 40 years/ and my ears are stupid/ when I run/ it is backward/ and the corridor is a rope above a mouth/ you come/ and you are singing that old song/ you're a bad dog baby/ but I still want you around/ the door opens/ and leads to a seaside town in winter/ on the edge of the world/ and beyond it/ is the great nothing I have become.

### *Body As Cemetery: An Extract from C+nto (Final Version)*

in sleep   my body is a haunted house   there are
footsteps along fallopian corridors   the corridor is a
rope strung above a mouth    I have been woken by
blurred voices   without bodies   quiet arguments in my
basement   once I was possessed   by a small girl   who
looked the same as me   who ate herself on a Sunday
afternoon   while her parents   downstairs   hardwired
their hangovers   & Christmas tunes   looped in nooses

//

my heart   is a church bell   but nobody visits   & God
is a man    hands in his pockets   watching.

//

## Can you tell me the origins of C+nto?

Apples & Snakes commissioned it while I was in Australia, as a twelve-to-thirteen-minute piece of immersive theatre to be performed at the Battersea Arts Centre, responding to the word 'protest'. It was during a distressing time in my life, and I didn't start thinking about it until I arrived in Singapore on the way home. I was on Facebook and discovered that a friend had died. This, combined with a rising negativity against lesbians and the LGBT+ community, led to an impulse of grief and anger at the way that my community was being lost. As soon as I started to think about it, people became ghosts, not necessarily because they were dead, but because they were no longer there.

The book is an ensemble piece. I went in with certain stories that needed to be told, but there are also composite characters merging elements of several people. I wanted to talk about women, to remember how hard women fought for their own space and also to explore the atemporality of everything through the mix of decades. The '*Vitrines*' in C+nto enabled me to create an imaginary world that would hold all of these disparate stories.

## It's quite an eye-catching title. How did it arise?

As it was originally written as a performance piece, which nobody was ever going to read, there wasn't a title, it was just called 'Rallying Cry'. In fact, I didn't write the titles for the specific sections of the poem until much later, I just had headings like Valentine 1, Valentine 2.

I showed the original version of 'Songs my Enemy Taught Me' to the poet Anthony Anaxagorou and he said, 'Cantos', to which I replied, 'No, 'Cuntos', it's all about women, darling'. This became a nickname for any time I wrote a set of cantos and then we discovered that it was a real word, meaning to recount a personal story, so it was both mildly offensive and absolutely accurate.

I didn't like it though, so I kept offering other titles, for example, '*The Heritages*'. I was trying to think of anything that was different to '*Cunto*', but my publisher, Saqi, loved '*Cunto*' so I said I'd use it if I could replace the '*u*' with the LGBT + sign. I got them to tweak '*other*' to '*othered*' too.

## Let's explore a small section of 'C+nto' in more detail.

This piece originated as a phone note and although it was initially called 'Body as Cemetery' it later became 'ROUND SIX the body as haunted house'. (The concept of rounds worked, as the performance was set in a boxing ring.)

The initial note is quite literal and narrates a true story. When I was about five, my father lost his job and that Christmas, we went to live in a bed and breakfast in Blackpool. I was sexually abused there and the image of the seaside town felt quite apocalyptic.

As I started to work on the poem, I wanted to bring out a more surreal aspect, so it became less centred on that single experience and those specific characters and more disembodied. Once I'd written '*the corridor is a rope above a mouth*', I knew where I was going as it had the haunting quality that I was seeking, whereas everything else in that first draft is very literal. As it developed, it became trippier and more depersonalised. The passive worked well with this and also served subconsciously as a method of disengaging from what had happened to me.

The slashes were replaced by gaps in order to replicate that sense of trauma and to emphasise the huge gaps in the narrative. The blank spaces on the page mirror the blank spaces in my mind.

The physical separation of the last two lines reflects the move from what happened to me, to the lack of intervention. The introduction of the church bell was important, signifying the aural as much as the visual reverberations. I don't have a religious background, but I was brought up in Lancashire where there was a strong Irish Catholic heritage and a sense of girls being punished under the guise of faith. God is a symbol both of patriarchy and the Catholic Church itself, and we are left with an image of society's voyeurism and inaction.

## How did your first version work as performance poetry?

There are three versions of '*C+nto*': a performance version which goes with the physical movements, a longer version and a published version.

Once I've established the world and what I want to say, I think of the pieces as films with a series of images. I strip back anything which might get in the way. It's very much about what an audience can follow, particularly as this is a thirteen-minute piece to perform and you're presenting lots of diverse information. This includes myriad surreal images and much anger. If it had just been written for the book version, it would have had a different shape and started in a different place.

I tried to make it fit the page better for the written version, paring it back, cutting out a lot of conjunctions, but there was also the opportunity to add different images, such as the '*tsunami quiff*', a '*shadow above the dreaming town*', tangential images that you're able to explore a little bit, which would have been too distracting in the performed version.

I'm trying to find a bridge between the spoken and written word, so that it doesn't become too obscure.

## This leads well into a discussion on some of the key differences between poetry and spoken word.

Poetry and spoken word differ in lots of ways, one of which is that you have more conclusions in spoken word. It's more finite as you're only hearing it once. We have that sense, when we're on stage in that live environment, that the audience wants an answer. It takes years to realise that the best poetry doesn't give any answers, it just asks questions. You must be absolutely clear with your images when it's for a live performance and you can't lose your rhythm, as the pace has to build up.

You can relax a bit more on the page and not worry about

following the same rhythms. There'll be places where it drops out and becomes a different meter. You can be more associative and extend images further; the worry here is about choosing the best words. With poetry you can leave a sense of wonder.

## Your performances seem very self-assured. Do you ever feel nervous?

Yes, it's terrifying. I'm a poet and poets aren't naturally gregarious, but I feel compelled. I came from a working-class background where nobody read literary magazines, so I didn't submit to them as I didn't speak the same language.

As nobody was ever going to read my work, I had to get up and say it or just give up. Early on in my career, I hid and told people shows had been cancelled so no one would come, and I wouldn't have to go on stage.

When I first performed '*C+nto*', I hadn't checked the contract carefully and only realised three days before the performance that I wasn't supposed to be reading it. I needed to memorise and perform the whole piece four times, back-to-back.

## I am interested in the fact that you reintroduced work from a previous poem in C+nto.

Yes, '*Some girls fall from sunlight skies grab their smiles from a hook behind the door,*' was taken from a piece which had previously appeared in '*Gutter Girls*'. When I originally had the idea for a book of cantos, I was going to begin every canto with those lines. I like the idea of the feminine morphology as a feminine aesthetic, the idea of extracting one thing from one poem and creating a whole new piece of work around that line, so it has this sense of a constant birthing of new things, so everything is inside everything else. In a way, it's a form of scaffolding.

## This poem uses research in order to go beyond your personal experiences.

As it's a memoir, my own lived experience provoked the research, which was then helpful in reminding me of other elements. I've always believed that it's very important to find the commonality between the personal and the global within my work, otherwise you're just writing reportage.

I was researching during lockdown, which was an interesting process. I finally got into the Bishopsgate Institute, in London, and when I opened a book, the flyers inside it immediately evoked the smell of the era.

## Do you have a writing routine?

To write, I need to be completely alone and completely silent. I'll say to everybody, 'I'm not coming out this week', so that means its twenty-four hours in which to write whenever I want. When I've been at my most tortured, like finishing my novel, *'The Night Alphabet'*, I might go to bed at 7pm, but be wide awake at midnight, ready to start work and then go to bed at 6am.

I use three mediums to write: handwritten notes, my phone and my laptop. Using kinaesthetically different media really helps my creative process. I think differently with a pen in my hand; I feel when I'm typing it's a different energy and different again on the mobile.

The first thing I do when I'm starting a new project is go through my phone for all of the lines I've kept. I write them on an A4 sheet on my laptop and carry on a line to see where it goes. Thus, the past is constantly feeding the future, but the future thinks differently so that the poem loses control of itself.

## Who was your favourite poet as a child?

Growing up, I didn't have much exposure to poetry. We weren't a family who had poetry books, but I remember my nan sharing Auden's *'Night Train'* with me and being caught up in her excitement. Then, as a fifteen-year-old, I found Wilfred Owen, who was meaningful to me.

However, most of all, I came to poetry through music and performance poets in the 80s, such as John Cooper Clarke, Linton Kwesi Johnson, Benjamin Zephaniah – and most importantly – Joolz (Jules Denby) who was the only woman in the UK practicing performance poetry at that time and a major influence.

## You often judge poetry competitions. What are you looking for?

I like surprises and I love that type of social surrealism, where a poem begins with a real issue, then slips into an extended metaphor through a surreal landscape. I think that women do this best. I like a poem in which the poet discovers themselves as they're writing it, they don't expect what they write.

## What advice would you offer to up and coming poets?

Read widely, don't just read poetry, read eclectically then, most importantly, let it all go. A poem is a conversation. It's difficult to create something wholly original, but that's the quest. It's a constant search for new things.

There's a theory that we all write about the same things until we die, everyone is circling the same issue, but we have to have some sense of moving forward too. We need to widen that orbit and go to new places with it.

The most important advice I can give you is to ask yourself the following questions. What are you trying to do? Do you want people to come together around an issue? Do you want them to see the craft of your poetry? What are your feelings about accessibility? If you want to write quite obscure poetry, whilst it'll reach some and that will be very important to you, be aware that it won't reach a lot of people. That's a decision you need to make.

Conversely, if you want to write hyper-accessible material, what does that mean about your ability to grow as a writer? When you know that, it will give you forward movement. As a writer I want to expose certain issues, which is a huge aspect of being part of a community to me. It's a powerful thing to have people come together to listen, and to then enable change.

# Biographies

**Mona Arshi**'s debut collection *'Small Hands'* won the Forward Prize for best first collection in 2015. Her second collection *'Dear Big Gods'* was published in 2019 (both books published by Liverpool University Press's Pavilion Poetry list). Her writing has been published in The Times, The Guardian, Granta, The Yale Review and The Times of India, as well as on the London Underground. She is currently a fellow in creative writing at Trinity College. Her debut novel *'Somebody Loves You'* was published by And Other Stories in 2021 and has been shortlisted for the Goldsmith Prize and Jhalak Prizes.

**Caroline Bird** is a poet and playwright. Her sixth collection, *'The Air Year'*, won the Forward Prize for Best Collection 2020 and was shortlisted for the Polari Prize and the Costa Prize. Her fifth collection, *'In These Days of Prohibition'*, was shortlisted for the 2017 TS Eliot Prize and the Ted Hughes Award. She won an Eric Gregory Award in 2002 and was shortlisted for the Geoffrey Dearmer Prize in 2001 and the Dylan Thomas Prize in 2008 and 2010. She was one of the five official poets at the 2012 London Olympics. As a playwright, Bird has been shortlisted for the George Devine Award and the Susan Smith Blackburn Prize. Her selected poems, *'Rookie'*, was published in May 2022.

**Regi Claire** Swiss-born, Edinburgh-based Regi Claire won the Mslexia/PBS Women's Poetry Competition 2019 and was a finalist for the Forward Prizes 2020 (Best Single Poem) and the Mslexia Women's Poetry Competition 2021. Her poems have appeared in numerous publications including *Ambit, Rialto, Best Scottish Poems 2021* and *Best New British and Irish Poets 2019-2021*. She is also the author of two novels and two short story collections. Her fiction has won a UBS Cultural Foundation award and has twice been shortlisted for Scotland's National

Book Awards. Regi teaches a course in critical reading at Edinburgh University.

**Gillian Clarke**, National Poet of Wales 2008-2016, President of Tŷ Newydd, the Welsh Writers Centre. In 2010 she was awarded the Queen's Gold Medal for Poetry. Her Selected Poems was published by Picador in 2016. In 2017 Carcanet brought out her tenth collection, *'Zoology'*, and her eleventh collection, *'The Silence'*, is due in Spring 2024. In 2021 Carcanet published *'Roots Home'*, essays and a journal, and Faber published her version of the 7th century Welsh poem, *'Y Gododdin, Lament for the Fallen'*. She lives on a smallholding in Ceredigion, where six acres have been planted with 4,500 native trees.

**Victoria Kennefick's** debut poetry collection, *'Eat or We Both Starve'* (Carcanet, 2021), won the Seamus Heaney First Collection Poetry Prize 2022 and the Dalkey Book Festival Emerging Writer of the Year Award 2022. It was shortlisted for the T.S. Eliot Prize, the Costa Poetry Book Award, Derek Walcott Prize for Poetry and the Butler Literary Prize. It was a book of the year in The Guardian, The Irish Times, The Telegraph, The Sunday Independent and The White Review. Victoria is UCD/Arts Council of Ireland Writer-in-Residence 2023 and Poet-in-Residence at the Yeats Society Sligo.

**Liz Lochhead** is a poet, playwright, performer and broadcaster. Her collections of poetry include *'Dreaming Frankenstein'*, *'The Colour of Black & White'*, *'A Choosing' (Selected Poems)*, *'Fugitive Colours'* and *'True Confessions'*, a collection of monologues and theatre lyrics. She served a five-year term as Scotland's Makar, or National Poet, from 2011 till 2016, and was awarded the Queen's Gold Medal for Poetry, 2015. In 2000 Liz was awarded Scotland's most prestigious book prize, The Saltire Society's Book of the Year Award, for the publication of her adaptation of Euripides' play *'Medea'*. In 2017 Liz won the Sunday Herald Scottish Culture Lifetime Achievement Award.

**Hannah Lowe** is a poet, memoirist and academic. Her latest book, *'The Kids'*, won the Costa Poetry Award and the Costa Book of the Year, 2021. Her first poetry collection *'Chick'* (Bloodaxe, 2013) won the Michael Murphy Memorial Award for Best First Collection. In September 2014, she was named as one of 20 Next Generation poets. Her family memoir *'Long Time, No See'* (Periscope, 2015) featured as Radio 4's Book of the Week. She is a Reader in Creative Writing at Brunel University.

**John McCullough**'s book of poems, *'Reckless Paper Birds'*, was published by Penned in the Margins. It won the 2020 Hawthornden Prize for Literature as well as being shortlisted for the Costa Poetry Award. His poem 'Flower of Sulphur' was shortlisted for the 2021 Forward Prize for Best Single Poem. His latest collection, *'Panic Response'*, was a Book of the Year in *The Telegraph* as well as being included in *The Times*' list of Notable New Poetry Books of 2022. He lives in Hove and teaches at the University of Brighton and for the Arvon Foundation.

**Kim Moore**'s pamphlet *'If We Could Speak Like Wolves'* was a winner in the 2011 Poetry Business Pamphlet Competition. Her first collection *'The Art of Falling'* (Seren 2015) won the Geoffrey Faber Memorial Prize. Her second collection *'All The Men I Never Married'* (Seren, 2021) won the 2022 Forward Prize for Best Collection. Her first non-fiction book *'What The Trumpet Taught Me'* was published by Smith/Doorstop in May 2022. She is a Lecturer in Creative Writing at Manchester Metropolitan University. A hybrid book of lyric essays and poetry *'Are You Judging Me Yet? Poetry and Everyday Sexism'* was published by Seren in March 2023.

**Sean O'Brien**'s eleventh collection of poems, *'Embark'*, was published by Picador in 2022. He is the recipient of awards including the T.S. Eliot and E.M. Forster and (three times) the Forward Prize. His translations include Dante's Inferno and the complete works of the Kazakh national poet Abai Kunanbayuli. His own work has been widely translated. He has written for the Royal National Theatre, for the RSC/ Live Theatre and for the ENO. He is also a novelist, short story writer and poetry critic. A Fellow of the Royal Society of Literature, he is Emeritus Professor of Creative Writing at Newcastle University.

**Don Paterson** is the author of sixteen books of poetry, aphorism, criticism, poetic theory and memoir. His poetry has won many awards, including the Whitbread Poetry Prize, the Geoffrey Faber Memorial Prize, the Costa Poetry Award, and three Forward Prizes; he is the only poet to have won the T.S. Eliot Prize on two occasions. He is Professor Emeritus at the University of St Andrews and for twenty-five years was Poetry Editor at Picador Macmillan. He is a Fellow of the English Association, the Royal Society of Literature, and the Royal Society of Edinburgh. He spent many years working as a jazz guitarist, and still regularly performs.

**Pascale Petit** was born in Paris and lives in Cornwall. She is of French, Welsh, and Indian heritage. Her eighth collection of poetry, *'Tiger Girl'*, was shortlisted for the Forward Prize and for Wales Book of the Year. Her seventh, *'Mama Amazonica'*, won the inaugural Laurel Prize, the RSL Ondaatje Prize, and was a Poetry Book Society Choice. Four previous collections were shortlisted for the T.S. Eliot Prize, including *'Fauverie'* (Seren, 2014), five poems from which won the Manchester Poetry Prize. Trained as a sculptor at the Royal College of Art, she spent the first part of her life as a visual artist.

**Jacob Sam-La Rose** is a poet, editor, facilitator and artistic director. He has been celebrated as a Change Maker by the Southbank Centre for 'changing the landscape of youth poetry in England'. Among other appointments, Jacob has served as a poetry professor at Guildhall School of Music and Drama, Poet-in-Residence at Raffles Institution (Singapore), and as the inaugural Poetry Fellow for English Heritage. His collection *'Breaking Silence'* was shortlisted for Fenton Aldeburgh and Forward Poetry prizes and is studied at A-level. He has been responsible for the Spoken Word Education Programme (Goldsmiths) and 12 Poets for 2012 (part of the Cultural Olympiad). He continues to lead Barbican Young Poets, which he established in 2009.

**George Szirtes** was born in Hungary, came to England as a refugee and trained as an artist. His twelfth book of poetry, *'Reel'* (2004) won the T S Eliot Prize for which he has been twice shortlisted since. His latest is *'Fresh Out of the Sky'* (2021). His memoir *'The Photographer at Sixteen'* (2019) was awarded the James Tait Black Prize in 2020. He is a co-winner of the International Booker translator's prize, as well as of numerous others. His own books have been translated into various languages including Italian, German, Chinese, Romanian and Hungarian.

**Joelle Taylor** is the author of 4 collections of poetry. Her most recent collection *'C+NTO & Othered Poems'* won the 2021 T.S Eliot Prize and the 2022 Polari Book Prize for LGBTQ authors. *'C+NTO'* is currently being adapted for theatre with a view to touring. She is a co-curator and host of Out-Spoken Live at the Southbank Centre, and tours her work internationally, from Australia to Brazil. Her novel of interconnecting stories *'The Night Alphabet'* will be published by riverrun in Spring of 2024. She is a Fellow of the Royal Society of Literature, and the 2022 Saboteur Spoken Word Artist of the Year.

## About the Editor

Rosanna McGlone is a writer and journalist. She has written more than 100 features for both national, and international, publications. Her first radio play was shortlisted for the BBC's Alfred Bradley Bursary Award. Her work has been supported by, amongst others, Arts Council England, The National Lottery Heritage Fund, Hull Truck Theatre, Vault Festival and The Old Vic New Voices Programme. Writing residencies include Capricorn Hill, NSW, Australia and The Hosking Houses Trust, Stratford-upon-Avon, England.

# Thanks

Sincere thanks to the following for their support: Arts Council England, without whom this book would not have been possible; Benjamin Zephaniah for his encouragement; Sarah Hosking and the Hosking Houses Trust for providing me with a room of my own; my son, Quin, for his input; my publisher, Isabelle Kenyon, at Fly on the Wall Press; the fantastic poets for making themselves vulnerable and believing in the book and, above all, my thanks to you, the reader, for being here.

# Acknowledgements

Thanks are due to the following for kind permission to reprint the poems included in this book:

Carcanet for permission to use Gillian Clarke's poem *'The Piano'* from *'Making the Beds for the Dead'*, Victoria Kennefick's poem *'Choke'* from *'Eat or We both Starve'* and Caroline's Bird's poem *'The Final Episode'* from *'The Air Year'*; Seren books for permission to republish Kim Moore's *'All thē Men I've ever Loved no. 42'* from *'All the Men I've ever Loved'* and Pascale Petit's *'Ortolan'* from *'Fauverie'*; Bloodaxe for *'The Register'* by Hannah Lowe from *'The Kids';* Saqi Books for *'ROUND 6 the body as haunted house'* by Joelle Taylor from *'C+nto and Othered Poems'*; Liverpool University Press for *'The Lion'* by Mona Arshi from *'Small Hands'*; Mslexia Magazine edition 84 for Regi Claire's *'(Un)certainties'*; Penned in the Margins for John McCullough's *'I've Carried a Door On My Back for Ten Years'* from *'Spacecraft'*; Pan McMillan for *'The Reader, after Daumier'* by Sean O'Brien from *'Embark'*; Faber for *'The Sicilian Advantage'* by Don Paterson from *'Arctic'*; Cristina Navazo-Eguía Newton, editor of *'Battered Moons Pamphlet 2018'* for Jacob Sam-La Rose's *'Credit Due'*.

# About Fly on the Wall Press

A publisher with a conscience.
*Political, Sustainable, Ethical.*
Publishing politically-engaged, international fiction, poetry and cross-genre anthologies on pressing issues. Founded in 2018 by founding editor, Isabelle Kenyon.

## Some other publications:

*The Sound of the Earth Singing to Herself by Ricky Ray*

*We Saw It All Happen by Julian Bishop*

*Odd as F*ck by Anne Walsh Donnelly*

*Imperfect Beginnings by Viv Fogel*

*These Mothers of Gods by Rachel Bower*

*Fauna by David Hartley*

*Snapshots of the Apocalypse by Katy Wimhurst*

*Demos Rising*

*Exposition Ladies by Helen Bowie*

*The House with Two Letterboxes by Janet H Swinney*

*Climacteric by Jo Bratten*

*The State of Us by Charlie Hill*

*In Conversation with… Small Press Publishers*

*The Finery by Rachel Grosvenor*

*The Sleepless by Liam Bell*

*The Unpicking by Donna Moore*

*The Naming of Moths by Tracy Fells*

Social Media:

@fly_press (X) @flyonthewallpress (Instagram)

@flyonthewallpress (Facebook)

www.flyonthewallpress.co.uk